Technician's Guide
to
Day Trading

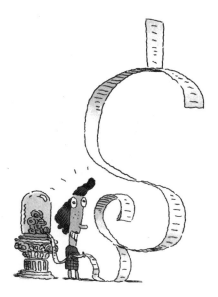

Technician's Guide
to
Day Trading

A Survival Guide for Profits and Sound Sleep

Martin J. Pring

International Institute for Economic Research, Inc.
1539 S. Orange Avenue   Sarasota, FL 34239
800-221-7514   941-364-5850   Fax: 941-364-9463

Web Site: www.pring.com

ISBN 0-9678691-1-0

Printed in the United States of America

1   2   3   4   5   6   7   8   9   0

Production work by Alchemy Designs, Inc.

Dust jacket, photo, book layout and design, CD interface and artwork by Alchemy Designs, Inc.

Printed and bound by Sheridan Books, Inc.

To my son Thomas William

My cherub and sunshine, boat buddy and pal

Acknowledgments

Among the folks to whom I am indebted for help in the preparation of this Tutorial CD and book, it would never have left the drawing board had it not been for several key people. A loving hug for my dedicated and stubborn wife who rewrote and painstakingly picked through my illegible manuscript changing all my many mistakes, typos and Olde English to a finished work. She accomplished all this while working a full day, tending to the kids, and supervising the renovation of our house by Bob, the carpenter. (Any mistakes that remain are, of course, my own responsibility.) As always, a big hug to Jimmie Sigsway, my wonderful mother-in-law (a.k.a. WGM - Worlds Greatest Mother-In-Law), who again spent hours proofing the proofed copy before it was proofed again. Also, a big thanks to Vivian Ivey, who proofread with a wicked blue pencil and reread Lisa's corrections and Pat Dickey, whose grammar is better than anyone's here.

I'm running out of dedications to Jeff Howard of Interactive Software Design, who, for the past seven years has, as usual, worked with us (sometimes a difficult and challenging task) often late in the evening and at the drop of a hat creating the install program and multimedia programming. I don't think I can say thanks enough for his dedication and friendship.

A special thanks goes to Chris Myers at Traders Library and Ed Dobson at Traders Press, who offered their support and encouragement in bringing this project to fruition. And lastly, thanks to my friends at Equis International (MetaStock), who generously allowed me to reproduce the charts that appear in the book and CD. ∎

Contents

Introduction

I n the last few years day trading has grown enormously in popularity. This has been due to technological gains which have allowed easy and much cheaper access to real time data feeds, dramatic declines in brokerage costs on the Internet and institutional changes on the NASDAQ and other exchanges that have leveled the playing field for individual investors. While day trading, like other forms of trading and investing, is likely to fluctuate with equity and other market cycles, it is definitely here to stay.

Up to now, most books on the subject have been concerned with the mechanics of day trading, and very little attention has been paid to the technical aspects; perhaps a token chapter on charts or some other technical concept. This presentation concentrates fully on market timing using the technical approach. I have assumed little or no technical knowledge by the reader and the concepts covered are pretty basic. However, even those experienced in the nuances of technical analysis will find some useful points of which they were not previously aware.

Many people associate day trading with a way of getting rich quickly with very little effort. While stories of traders making it "big" often find their way to the headlines, for most of us living in the trenches, nothing could be further from the truth. Advertisements by brokers and others with a vested interest in making money from the unwary trader also add to the mystique. Make no mistake about it though; day trading is not a fast track to instant wealth. In fact, more people lose their capital in the first year of trading than manage to make it grow. We never hear of these stories in the media because it is not news; and it certainly does not make good copy for advertisers anxious for you to pay them money.

These remarks are intended to calm your enthusiasm for day trading, not eliminate it. If you approach trading as a business rather than a hobby, you are much more likely to be successful. Day trading, just like any other venture, requires knowledge and discipline in its application. I have always believed the key to

---

success is knowing and doing. This book can certainly help in the "knowing" part, but actually applying the knowledge learned requires patience and discipline, and there is only one person who can apply it…. and that's you!!

One of the biggest mistakes made by neophyte traders is that they go for the big kill. Sometimes this works, but rarely more than once. If you are lucky enough to make a home run, it is usually due literally to luck. Professionals know the odds are against them and do not put their trust in luck. They typically harvest profits, taking some here, giving back a little there. In many cases, they actually lose more times than they win, but the operation is profitable because these savvy traders cut losses quickly. They instantly recognize when the market moves against them and get out. In this way, their average win is far greater than the average loss and they become successful.

The bulk of this book has been devoted to technical analysis concepts, but I have also included three chapters on trading tactics and psychological aspects. These are intended as starting points for the application of those very important concepts of patience and discipline. After all, you can have all the knowledge in the world, but if you fail to apply it correctly, it will not benefit you whatsoever. With these thoughts in mind, please enjoy the book, remembering at all times that technical analysis, like all the other investment disciplines, is far from perfect. But by applying it diligently, it will definitely put the odds in your favor.

With all this in mind, enjoy the material, learn the rules and principles that are covered here, and most of all, good luck and good charting! ∎

Martin J. Pring

Technician's Guide
to Day Trading

Chapter 1 ————————————————

Decisions
You Must Make

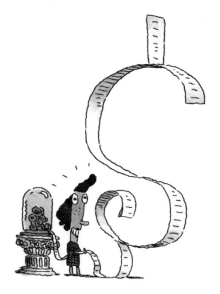

Introduction to Day Trading

Day trading has recently become the latest fad in the trading world, growing by leaps and bounds in popularity. The only difference between day trading and other forms of trading, though, is the **time horizon**. Instead of taking positions home for several days or weeks, day traders typically buy and sell securities throughout the day, often liquidating everything before the session ends. The same requirements longer-term traders use—establishing a methodology and applying patience and discipline—still apply whatever the time frame. If anything, day trading requires more focus, since things can and do happen much, much faster. Trading off the long-term fundamentals is not an option with day traders since they change over a relatively long period of time unless, of course, prices change due to unexpected corporate developments within the trading session. So, in order to be successful, the day trader must rely on technical factors. These technical factors can take the form of actual charts featuring indicators with a greatly reduced time frame, or what we might call "the tape reading street smart approach". In this method, traders watch the tape and the market's response to news rather than the charts themselves. If bad news fails to depress a stock, then it is unlikely to go down, indicating short positions should be covered and the stock should, perhaps, be purchased. Day traders also study certain relationships to gauge the subtle strengths and weaknesses of emerging trend changes from which they can profit. An example of a sign of strength would be if technology *stock*s have been particularly weak and the market moves to a new low, but the technology *leaders do not*.

In this tutorial, we will principally be concerned with the chart reading approach. However, tape reading and market savvy aspects will also be covered.

To Overnight or Not Overnight

I mentioned earlier that a lot of traders liquidate their positions at the end of a session. There are pluses and minuses to this approach. On the one hand, it is a good idea not to be exposed overnight, since events can, and do, change between the close and the next day's opening. **Gaps**, or holes can appear in the chart as in Chart 1.1 of a 5-minute bar chart of corn. If you do not take home a **position overnight** it means that you have to monitor the next day's activity and then come to a conclusion before a new position can be entered. In the process, valuable opportunities may be lost. Alternatively, enough time may not have elapsed to provide an accurate view of what is really going on. In effect, the trading decisions are being forced on the trader by artificial time constraints.

On the other hand, if positions are taken home overnight, it is possible to take advantage of larger trends since markets often begin the next day moving in the general direction they finished the day before. In this case, larger trends are classified as those lasting for a day or two.

You will find that I change between these purely intraday examples and charts of intraday data that span several days, sometimes longer. Even if you are not a true day trader; i.e., one who does not take a position home, the intraday charts can still be

Chart 1.1   Corn 5-minute Bar

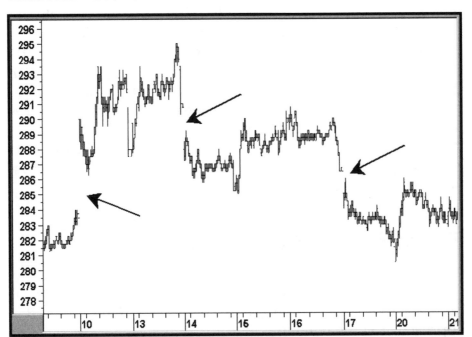

Chart 1.2 S&P Composite (Weekly Data)

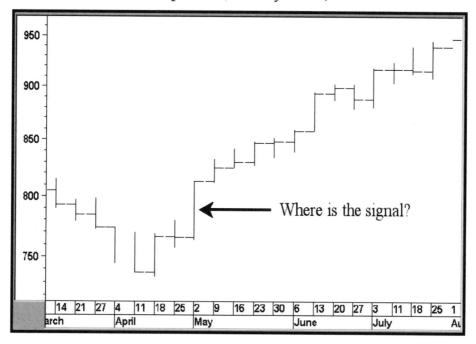

of great use. Chart 1.2 shows weekly data for the S&P Composite. The early May rally is not signaled by any serious trendline break or price pattern formation. However, when we look at the same information expressed in a daily format in Chart 1.3, we can see a **reverse head and shoulders** formation. In this example, the weekly chart was used to gain perspective, but the daily one provided us with more timely clues concerning emerging trends. If you are not familiar with the term "reverse head and shoulders", do not worry. This type of formation, along with other price patterns, is covered at length in a subsequent chapter.

This idea of using charts with short-term time frames can also be used with the intraday daily relationship. Chart 1.4 contains daily data for December 1997 corn—not really much to report here. However, the exact same period using a 5-minute bar chart is also shown in Chart 1.5. Here it is apparent that the price decline for December 1997 corn on the 16th was preceded by the completion and breakdown from a top formation. Once again, the intraday chart provided us with the kind of detail to help us get positioned for longer-term trades.

Chart 1.3   S&P Composite (Weekly Data)

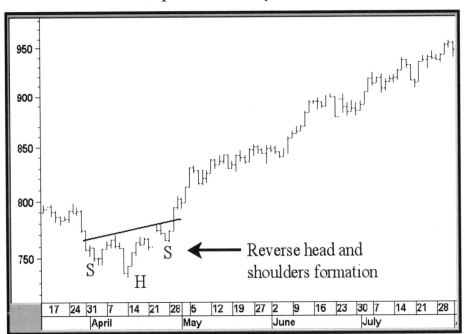

Time Frames

Intraday charts can be broken down into many different **time frames**. The smallest is the tick (Chart 1.6). This is where every trade is recorded and plotted accordingly, as the price level changes. The problem using **tick charts** is that by the time you realize what is happening, activity on the trading floor may be totally different due to the time delay of reporting, charting, and the placement of an order to your broker and then to the floor. For this reason, it is probably wiser to use a 5-minute chart (Chart 1.7), as the minimum time frame. A 5-minute chart means a new bar is plotted every five minutes containing the opening high, low, and close for each 5-minute interval. This is similar to a daily chart, which includes the same information, but it is spread over the entire trading session.

I also think that 15-minute, 30-minute, and hourly charts are

Chart 1.4   December 1997 Corn (Daily Data)

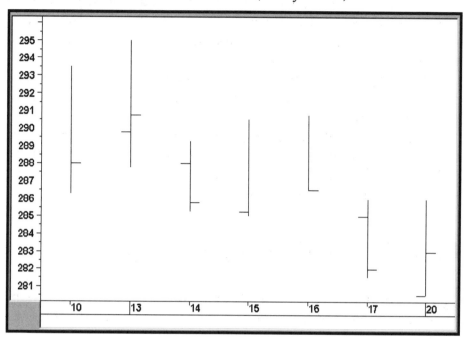

Chart 1.5   Corn 5-minute Bar

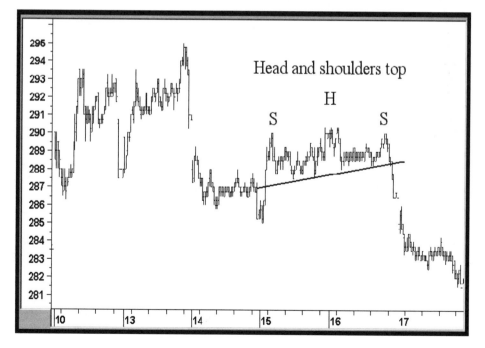

very useful because they display more data during the trading day. If you used longer time spans, it would not be possible to identify any meaningful trends. I also believe that 5 -minute charts give you a broader perspective, though there are many who would disagree with this statement.

Deciding on a time frame is very much up to you. Try experimenting with several, ending up with the one that feels the most comfortable and works for you.

Always remember, though, that however small a time frame you decide to work with, you should always (yes, always!), be mindful of the *direction of the trend as measured by longer time frames* since this will give you perspective.

Establishing a Trading Strategy

A **trading strategy** is the driving force behind the decision-making process. Before you can enter any trade, you must have a

Chart 1.6   Corn Tick

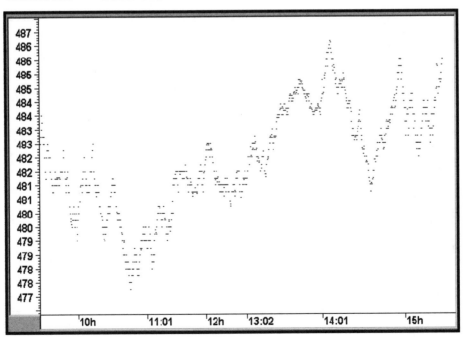

Chart 1.7   Corn 5-minute Bar

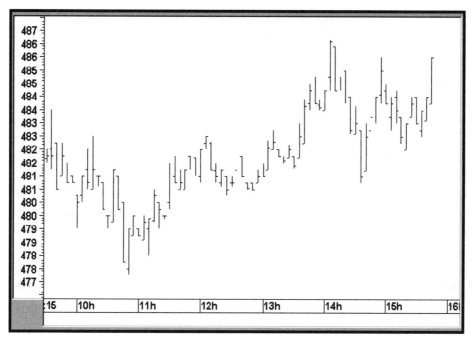

justification for buying/selling—other than a gut feeling that the price is going to rise or fall. This rationalization should be based on a methodology or trading strategy with which you feel comfortable. This could be as simple as buying higher highs and selling lower lows, or a complex integration of a moving average crossover/oscillator overbought/oversold analysis. The important point to remember is that <u>you must apply a technique that helps you make decisions in a methodical and impartial way</u>. At this point, you probably have no idea what that might be. The goal of this tutorial is to offer ideas to help you develop your own personal technique.

Risk Management

Perhaps the least understood principle of trading for those entering the arena for the first time is the concept of **risk management**. We are all quick to think of profits, but few of us concentrate on losses. Yet, **managing losses** is the first and most important step we have to take. After all, if you lose your capital you are out of the game. Limiting risk and quickly taking losses will allow you to come back time and time again. Table 1.1 is very instructive since it shows that recovering from large losses can be very difficult. Here you can see that the starting amount of capital is $100. The first trade loses 50%, or $50, and leaves an ending balance of $50, to begin the next trade. The second trade increases by 50%, or $25 and leaves us with an ending balance of $75. The next three trades each make 10%. This gives us a total gain in four trades of 80%... compared to the one loss of 50%. Unfortunately, even with all of this smart trading, we are still a fraction under our starting capital. When we bear in mind that successful traders expect more losing than profitable trades, you can appreciate the 50% loss is pretty difficult to come back from. In this example, we had four winners and one loser, which is way above the norm. You will almost certainly find you make more losing than winning trades, so it is very important to cut losses and let profits run. Whenever you enter a trade you should always ask the questions: What is my likely reward and what is my potential risk? If

Table 1.1   The Importance of Managing Losses

	Capital	Profit/Loss %	Profit/Loss Amount	Ending
Trade 1	100	(50)	(50)	50
Trade 2	50	50	25	75
Trade 3	75	10	75	82.5
Trade 4	82.5	10	83	90.8
Trade 5	90.8	10	9.1	99.9

the reward does not exceed the risk by a comfortable margin the trade should not be executed.

Using Money Management Techniques

Since day trading involves leverage, **money management** involves the optimum allocation of capital to a margined position. This means you should not put all of your money at risk for one or two trades. Allocate a small amount of capital first and learn to lose money, gaining from that experience in small doses. Once you become more confident in your approach, you can extend the amount of capital at risk a little more, but never more than 10% at a time.

A golden rule of day trading is to take money out of the markets in small amounts—never go for broke and try to make a home run by placing big bets. The reasons for this are: First, this will totally kill you emotionally, causing you to lose the most important element of investment psychology—objectivity. Second, you might win once, or even twice, but eventually the markets will catch up with this "gun slinging" technique and wipe you out. ■

Chapter 2

Peak and Trough
Analysis

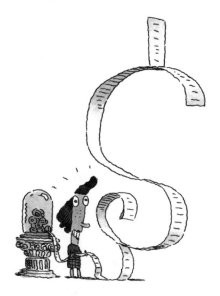

Defining the Trend

Technical analysis assumes prices move in **trends**, and that once a trend begins, it tends to perpetuate. Most all of the work done in technical analysis is concerned with trying to identify when trends reverse so new positions can be entered, or old ones reversed. All of the techniques covered in this book will better help you identify when these trends reverse, how to buy into an area where they might reverse, or sell at a price where a decline could be expected. These points, known as support and resistance, will be covered at length in Chapter Three. The tools used in technical analysis are all aimed at identifying trend reversals at an early stage. Since trends *have a tendency to perpetuate, we ride on those trends until the weight of the evidence shows or proves that the trend has reversed.* The weight of the evidence in this case refers to the number of reliable technical indicators that are all pointing in the same direction. Remember, the greater the number of indicators, the greater the probabilities of a reversal. I use the word "probabilities" because **technical analysis deals with odds and probabilities that things are about to change.** Unfortunately, there is no known method of forecasting the duration and magnitude of a trend with any degree of consistency—identifying reversals is hard enough.

Three Important Trends

You may be asking yourself the question, "What is a trend and how long does it last?" There are countless numbers of trends, but before the advent of intraday charts, there were three generally accepted durations: primary, intermediate and short-term.

The **main,** or **primary trend** (Figure 2.1), is often referred to as a bull or bear market. Bulls go up and bears go down. They typically last about nine months to two years with bear market troughs separated by just under four years. These trends revolve around the business cycle and tend to repeat whether the weak phase of the cycle is an actual recession, or if there is no recession and just slow growth.

Figure 2.1 Primary Trend

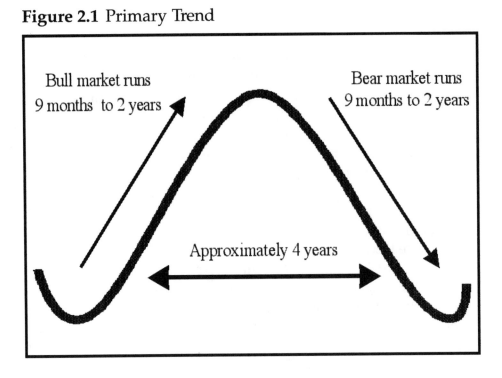

Bull market runs
9 months to 2 years

Bear market runs
9 months to 2 years

Approximately 4 years

Primary trends are not straight-line affairs, but are a series of rallies and reactions. These series of rallies and reactions (Figure 2.2) are known as **intermediate trends**. They can vary in length from as little as six weeks to as much as nine months, or the length of a very short primary trend. Intermediate trends typically develop as a result of changing perceptions concerning economic, financial, or political events. It is important to have some understanding of the direction of the main or primary trend because rallies in bull markets are strong and reactions are weak. On the other hand, reactions in bear markets are strong and rallies are short, sharp, and generally, unpredictable. If you have a fix on the underlying primary trend, you will be better prepared for the nature of the intermediate rallies and the reactions that will unfold. In turn, intermediate trends can be broken down into **short-term trends**, which last from as little as two weeks to as much as five or six weeks. They are shown in Figure 2.2 by the dashed lines.

Since all three trends discussed are shown in Figure 2.2, there are a couple of points worth making. First, as an investor, it is

Figure 2.2 Market Cycle Model

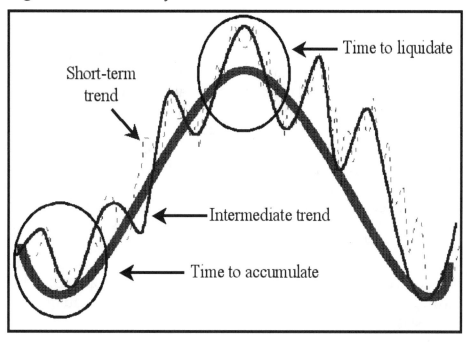

best to accumulate when the primary trend is in the early stages of reversing from down to up, and liquidate when the trend is reversing from up to down. Second, as traders, we are better off if we position ourselves with the long side in a bull market since that is when short-term uptrends tend to have the greatest magnitude. By the same token, it does not usually pay to short in a bull market because declines can be quite brief and reversals to the upside unexpectedly sharp. If you are going to make a mistake, it is more likely to come from a counter-cyclical trade.

You may think all of this takes us a long way from intraday charting, but not really. It is important to remember that even on intraday charts, the predominant trend determines the magnitude and duration of the shorter moves. You may not feel a three-hour rally is closely related to a two-year primary bull market move, but it is just as related as a five or six-day trend. Later, in Chapter 11 featuring the KST, we will examine these types of intraday relationships in closer detail.

Peak and Trough Analysis

It is a fact that prices rarely move in a straight line. Rather, they form a steady pattern of rising **peaks and troughs** in an uptrend and declining peaks and troughs in a downtrend. This principal building block of technical analysis appears to be especially true for intraday charts, and is well worth considering as a legitimate technique for day trading.

Figure 2.3 shows a series of rising peaks and troughs—a normal uptrend. It becomes apparent at point (A) that the latest peak is lower than its predecessor. Thus, the series of rising peaks is no longer intact, but the series of rising troughs is. It is not until the price breaks below the previous low at (B), that a series of declining peaks and troughs is signaled.

Figure 2.4 shows a declining market, where the process is reversed. The price fails to take out the final low at point (C). This indicates that a reversal may be underway, but an actual trend reversal signal is not triggered until it subsequently rallies above

Figure 2.3 Normal Uptrend

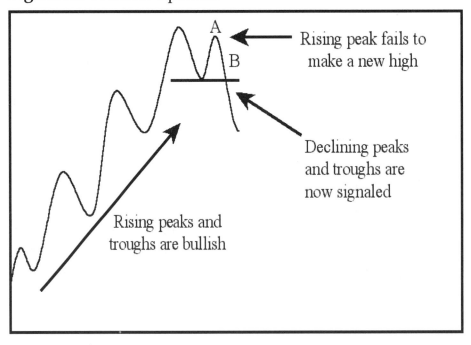

Figure 2.4 Declining Market

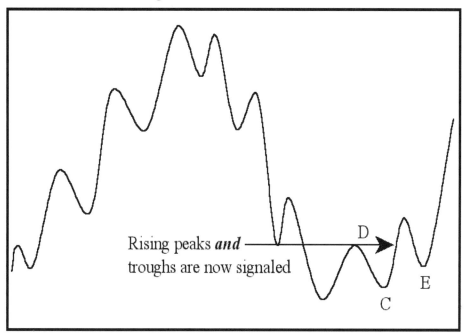

Rising peaks *and* troughs are now signaled

D

C

E

the previous high at point (D). Since this is a peak/trough progression, it should not be surprising that the price falls below (D) again. However, as long as it remains above the previous trough the rising trend of peaks and troughs is still intact and the trend continues to be classified as bullish.

Learning the Half Signals

We are occasionally left in doubt as to whether a trend has reversed or not. In Figure 2.5, we see that at point (X) the latest trough breaks below its predecessor, but not the latest peak. At point (X) we are limited to only a **half signal**. What is now required is for a fresh rally to peak out below the previous top and for the price to slip below the previous low at point (Y). This is obviously a much less timely signal because the price has already fallen a long way from the final high, but the probabilities of a reversal are much greater. After all, Figure 2.6 shows what could

Figure 2.5 Upside Reversal

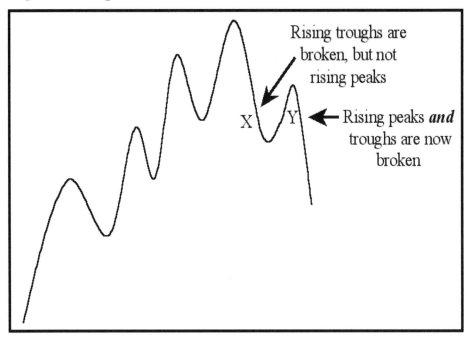

Figure 2.6 Non-Signal

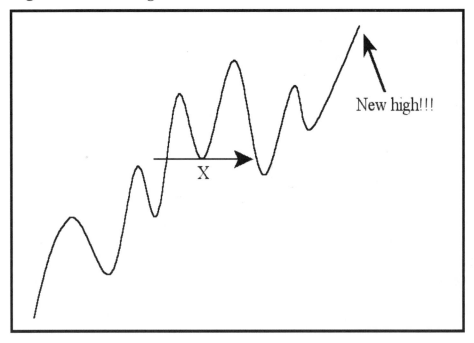

have happened next; the price rises and makes a new peak, indicating the trend was never reversed in the first place!

Lines / Consolidations

Occasionally, reactions within a trend develop as a sideways movement where the price experiences a trading range. In Figure 2.7, it is consolidating gains during the ranging action and, in Figure 2.8, it is digesting losses. These **trading ranges** are also known as **lines**, as originally termed in *Dow Theory*. Whenever the price experiences a breakout from a trading range, such as these, it has the same effect as if the range was a rally or reaction. This means that it is possible for a breakout from a trading range to either act as a peak and trough buy or sell signal, as in Figure 2.9, or a reconfirmation of the prevailing trend, as in Figure 2.10.

Figure 2.7   Consolidating Gains During Ranging Action

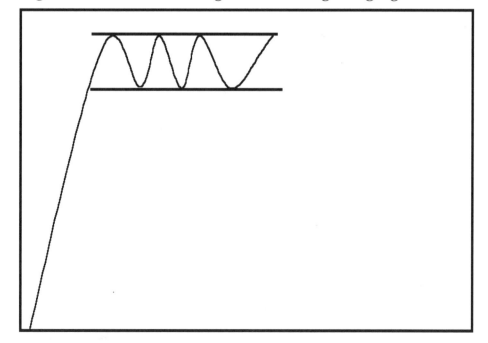

Figure 2.8 Digesting Losses During Ranging Action

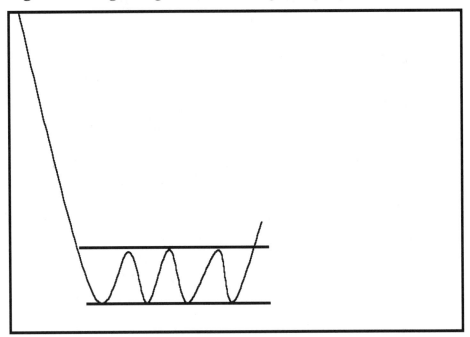

Figure 2.9 Breakout Acting As Buy or Sell Signal

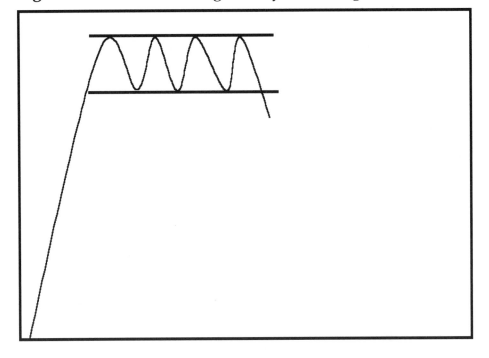

Figure 2.10 Reconfirmation of the Prevailing Trend

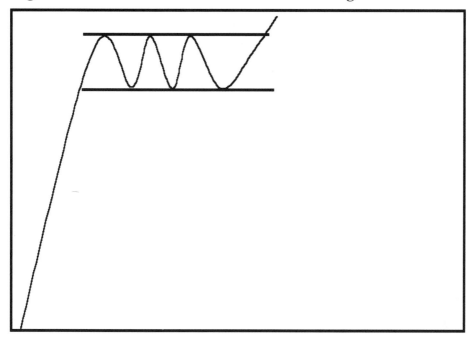

What Constitutes a Legitimate Peak and Trough?

Most of the time, the various rallies and reactions are self-evident, so it is easy to determine that these turning points are legitimate peaks and troughs. Technical lore has it that a reaction to the prevailing trend should retrace between one to two-thirds of the previous move. Thus, in Figure 2.11, the first rally from the trough low to the subsequent peak is 100%. The ensuing reaction appears to be just over 1/2 or a 50% retracement of the previous move. Occasionally, the retracement can reach 100%. Technical analysis is far from precise, but if a retracement move is a good deal less than the minimum 1/3 retracement, then the peak or trough in question is held to be suspect.

You can appreciate that a line is a fairly controlled period of profit taking, or digestion of losses. The depth of the trading range

Figure 2.11 "Legitimate" Peak and Trough

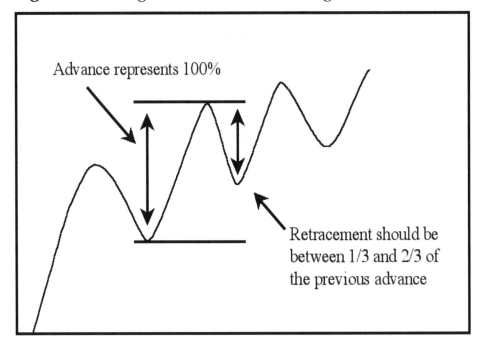

can fall short of the minimum "approximate one-third retracement" requirement and, in such instances, the correction qualifies more on the basis of time than magnitude. A rule of thumb might be for the correction to last between one- and two-thirds of the time taken to achieve the previous advance or decline. In Figure 2.12, the distance between the low and the high for the move represents 100%. The consolidation prior to the breakout constitutes 2/3 or 66% of the time taken to achieve the advance— ample time to consolidate gains and move on to a new high. These are only rough guidelines and in the final analysis, it is a judgment call based on experience, common sense, a bit of intuition, and perhaps most important of all, a review of other factors such as volume, support and resistance principles, etc. We have mainly been studying these concepts in a rising trend. However, the principles work exactly the same in a declining trend in that rallies should retrace 1/3 to 2/3 of the previous decline.

These diagrams make it pretty clear what constitutes a peak and trough, but in the real world, things are not always so clearcut. Let's look at an example of the S&P Composite.

Figure 2.12 Formation of a Line

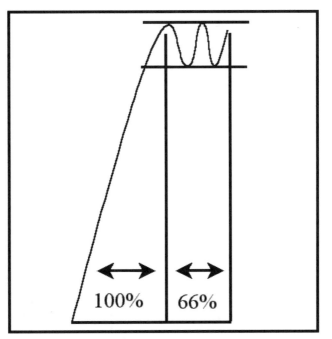

Marketplace Examples, Part I

Chart 2.1 features a 10-day intraday bar chart derived from the popular Telescan® *TIP@Wallstreet* charting software. The action opens on Tuesday, which establishes a rally and reaction. At this point, the direction of the trend is not yet known. The market rallies on the Wednesday opening, so the Tuesday low (A) becomes a reference low. If the current rally fails to take out the Tuesday high (B) and the price then falls below the late Tuesday low (A), a downtrend will be confirmed. As time progresses, the price does fail to make a new high, but at the same time, the decline has managed to hold above the late Tuesday low (A). The Wednesday high (C) now becomes our reference peak and takes the place of the Tuesday high (B). A few more hours elapse and there is still no resolution to the problem. Consequently, it is assumed that the downtrend is still in force since no signal of a reversal has yet been given. This is a wise conclusion, since the early Thursday morning rally fails to improve on the Wednesday peak, and by

Chart 2.1 S&P Composite 5-minute Bar

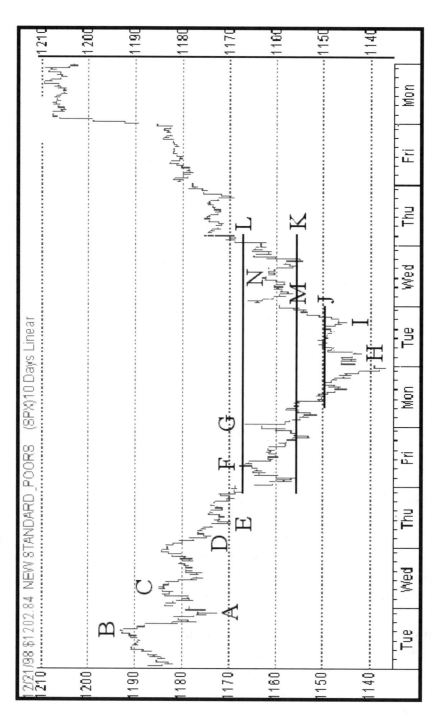

mid-morning Thursday the price has broken below the mid-Wednesday low (D). Then it takes out the original Tuesday low (E) and continues declining. It gaps down on Friday morning and by the middle of the day, a rally closes most of the opening gap (F). Our reference point for a new rally high remains at the late Wednesday high around 1,183, and that is quite far away. Even if it were bettered on the upside we would still need to see a series of rising troughs in order to get a good signal. Since the Friday bottom is the low for the move, such a development is not in the cards at this time. If the Friday opening were to be the turning point, we would need to see a reaction and a successful test of that low. In fact, it does not matter that much because the price subsequently goes on to register a new low. This is good news, in a way, because the reference high now becomes the mid-day Friday peak (F), down from the 1,183 level of late Wednesday. The price then rallies (G), but is unable to take out the mid-Friday high, so the series of declining peaks is still in force.

The price now moves to a new low and then starts to bounce. The first reaction tries to close Tuesday's opening gap at (H). However, it does not really qualify as a low from the point of view of a trend reversal signal since it does not contain much magnitude, and only lasts for a short period. The Tuesday afternoon reaction is not much greater (I), but it becomes a new reference low for two reasons. First, if it holds, we would have a series of possible mini-rising bottoms. More importantly, the Tuesday afternoon decline begins from the same level as the early Monday afternoon setback at the trendline marked by letter (J). This 1,150/1,151 area is clearly resistance, so when the price breaks above it to make a new high, it is classified as a trend reversal signal. Our sell stop is now entered just below the Tuesday afternoon reaction low (I) at about 1,145.

If a rally phase is now assumed, it is reasonable to ask where the next level of resistance lies so we can either be prepared to take profits when the price gets there, or alternatively, where we need to place a sell order. There are two possibilities. The first is at (K), which marks the early Friday low set on the way down, and is at roughly the same level as the small mid-Monday advance. The second possibility is at the Friday and early Monday highs (L). This one is much better since it also occurs at the start of the Friday opening gap. As it turns out, this is precisely where the rally ends. The resistance level at (L) and the subsequent low at (M), become our new reference points, so the sell stop is raised again to (M). This is a good support area since it was the lower resistance zone that we picked earlier; i.e., the lower dashed line at (K). A break below the line should give us a valid signal that the trend has reversed to the downside. As you can see, it did and a new low was registered. If we were trading from both the long and short side, a sell stop would be placed just above the mid-Wednesday high (N). We are stopped out almost immediately as the price quickly reverses direction and advances above the mid-Wednesday high—so much for the "valid" signal. Unfortunately, markets can and do change their mind, and I was fairly certain that a decline would take place so, as a trader, I must also respect the market when it goes against my expectations.

At this point, we have rising peaks and declining troughs. Clearly the evidence is contradictory, so the rule is "when in doubt, stay out." In effect, I liquidate the short position, but do not go long because the direction of the trend is now unclear. If it reverses once again and immediately breaks below the whipsaw low just below (K), the series of rising peaks will still be intact, so it would be unwise to go short. On the other hand, if it breaks above the early Wednesday high (N), the series of declining troughs will be intact. Can we go long based on that? No, not really. However, it is apparent that if the price does rally above the line at (L), the new high will also take out the previous four peaks. This will represent an important signal in its own right. Therefore, it is possible to justify buying on a half-signal, since the purchase is based more on the breakout than the peak and trough technique. The sell stop would be placed just below the late Wednesday congestion range since a decline below the line at (L) would indicate the probabilities of a false breakout. This turned out to be a lucky move since the price went on to make significant new highs.

Marketplace Examples, Part II (Microsoft)

Chart 2.2 features an intraday bar chart for Microsoft. It is not as easy to apply peak and trough techniques on this chart as the previous example using the S&P Composite, since the days in-

Chart 2.1 S&P Composite 5-minute Bar (Repeated)

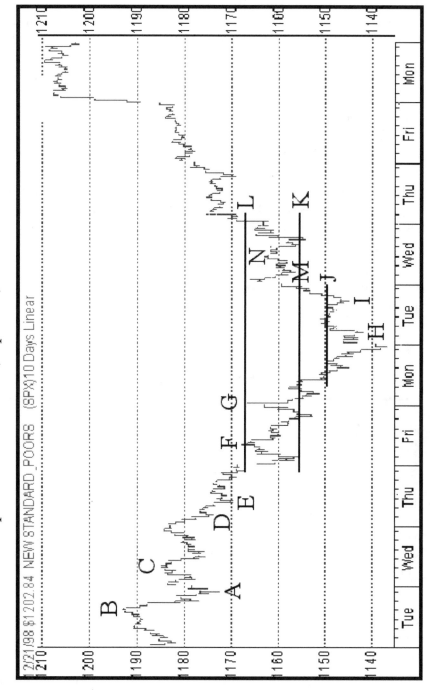

cluded in the rectangle covered a trading range environment. It is often a good idea to display charts on a line, or close-only basis. In this way, the rallies and reactions often become more clear. Chart 2.3 displays the same information, but this time on a closing basis. As trading begins, you can see the price actually traced out a series of rising peaks and troughs until the opening on Friday (A). The high for the move was attained close to the session's end on Thursday, but by the opening (B), the low for the next decline takes the price below its early Thursday morning bottom. This broke the series of rising bottoms, but not, of course, the rising peaks. The next rally (C) took the price back marginally above the Thursday high. The next low returned it back to support in the $132 area and it was not until a subsequent weaker rally and decline to a new low took place that a new downtrend was signaled at D. This break was also important because the decline took out the previous four bottoms.

The subsequent decline was sharp, but short-lived. The next buy signal would have been triggered when the price broke above the sideways consolidation late on Tuesday afternoon (E). While

Chart 2.2   Microsoft 15-minute Bar

Chart 2.3 Microsoft 15-minute Bar

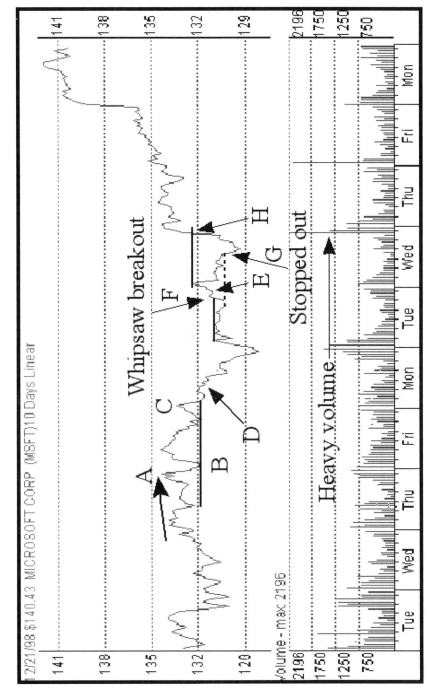

the sideways movement does not strictly qualify as a decline, it is a corrective movement and qualifies under the Dow Theory as a line. The question now would be, "Where is the next level of resistance?" The answer, quite obviously, is the $132 area, which was previously one of support. Had I bought on the basis of the break above the consolidation, I would place my protective stop just a little underneath. As luck would have it, the price rallied just a little bit above $132. As you can see, the buy was a whipsaw (F) and the position was liquidated for a small loss at (G). I am now left with a cash position since the chart, at this point, is once again experiencing rising peaks and declining bottoms in a similar manner to what we saw in the previous chart. Once again, at this point, there are no benchmarks that could reliably be expected to signal a downside breakout. Therefore, it is better to do nothing. On the other hand, a rally above $132 will take out the early Wednesday peak, which, as we have already said, represents important resistance. As you can see, the price did rally above this point and stopped us in at (H). The breakout is very convincing since it is accompanied by exceptional volume. The question now facing us is, "Where to place the protective stop?" If it is put under the previous mid-Wednesday low it will involve a $3 risk, which is too much. In fact, it could be greater than $3 because this chart is based on the closing price for the bar. It is actually better to place the stop just under the breakout point around $131.50. After all, the position was really acquired on the basis of the breakout. This means that if the breakout fails, the market is not acting as expected, so the position should be liquidated. After the breakout, the price experiences a small pull back. This could be regarded as a legitimate correction where a reference low could be established; however, it fell far short of the normal 1/3 to 2/3 retracement of the previous move. Also, the next rally took the price to a new high, so even though the subsequent bottom was marginally lower, the series of rising peaks was still intact at that point. We still had our stop just under the $132 support area, so a little nail biting would have taken place over the next few hours. As it turned out, this was the thing to do, since the price experienced a spirited rally into midday Monday. ■

Chart 2.3 Microsoft 15-minute Bar (Repeated)

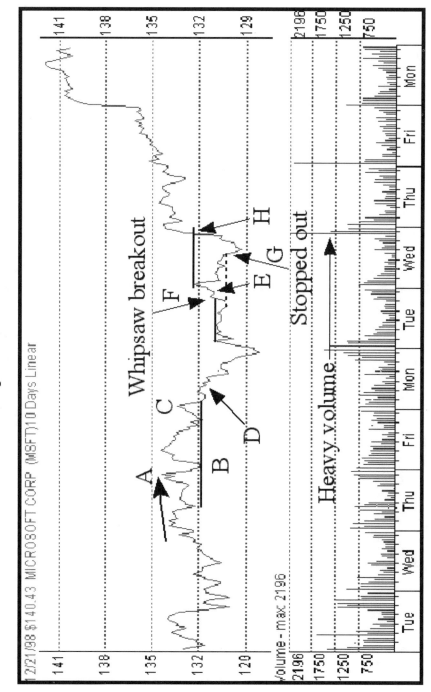

Chapter 3

Support
and Resistance

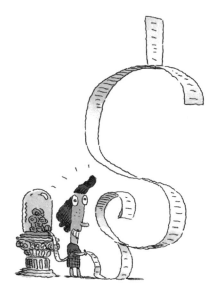

Introduction

Support and resistance are terms we hear bandied about quite a lot, but to many of us their meaning is quite vague. Quite often, seasoned pros say "resistance" when they actually mean to say support, and "support" when they really mean resistance; it is no wonder there is a lot of confusion.

Basically, support and resistance are points on a chart where the probabilities favor a halt or even a reversal in the prevailing trend. **Support** is where a declining trend can be expected to halt temporarily due to a concentration of demand. **Resistance** is where an advancing trend can be expected to halt temporarily due to a concentration of supply.

In Figure 3.1, the price falls to (A), and then bounces. We now know that at point (A), selling dries up and buying becomes stronger, so (A) is now deemed a support area. Also, at point (A), we have a concentration of demand. Obviously demand and supply are always equal, so the concentration of demand means that

Figure 3.1 Support Violation

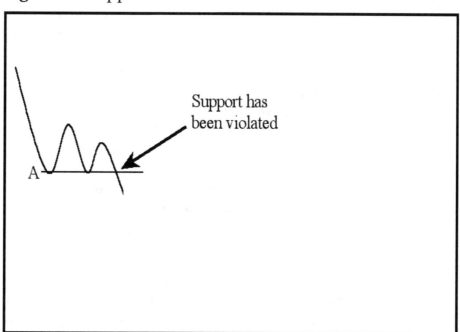

buyers are more enthusiastic than sellers and are therefore more willing to bid up prices. If prices reverse and start to decline again, it would be reasonable to expect (A) to continue to provide support. As it turned out, selling dried up again and prices rallied for a second time. When the next sell-off takes place, the price is unable to hold at (A) and we say the support level was violated. Think of support like this: If you jump up and down on the tenth floor of an old and decrepit multi-story building, eventually the floor gives way. The floor was your support area, which has now been violated. Thinking of personal safety, you must now look out for the next area of support, which is the floor of the ninth story. The same is true in markets; when a particular support level is violated you need to look for the next one down.

In this instance, there is no history of prior declines, so there is no evident support level until the price falls to (B) and then bounces (Figure 3.2). After a rally, (B) gives way and a new level of support is established at (C). In this case, the price bounces several times from the support zone. The more times it bounces from (C), the greater its importance. Every time the price falls to (C), buyers become more enthusiastic than sellers because they feel the security in question is a bargain. Sellers, for their part, think that the price is too low and are prepared to wait for higher prices. Notice, though, that every time the price rises, it seems to get turned back at the same point. This is a concentration of supply and is known as **resistance**. This relatively higher level of prices attracts the sellers who were reluctant to liquidate at (C). At the same time, the bargain hunter buyers at (C) are less enthusiastic at the line and wait for another opportunity to buy at (C). If you look carefully, you will see the resistance level formed at approximately the same level as the support at (B). This is important because it is a rule of technical analysis that **what becomes support on the way down, turns out to be resistance on the way up.** Just remember our analogy of falling through the tenth floor and finding support at the ninth. If you want to get back to the tenth, you are going have to jump through the ceiling of the ninth floor because that now becomes resistance; it is the same in the markets.

Eventually, the resistance level is violated and prices advance to the next level of resistance, which is back at (A) in Figure 3.3. Once again, the previous level of support on the way down is

Figure 3.2 Support/Resistance Reversal Role

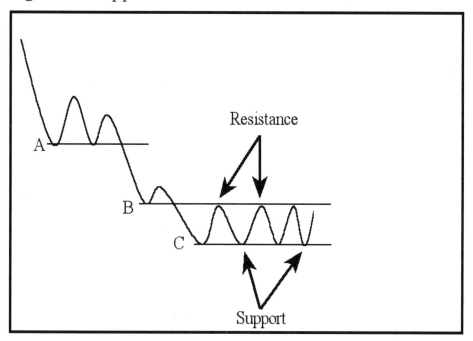

reversed to a level of resistance on the way up. The rationale for this lies in the fact that quite a few people bought at (A), and when the price broke below it, they ended up with a paper loss. Now that the price has returned to the area of (A) again, they have the chance to break even so a lot of them take advantage of the opportunity and sell. You will also find that once a resistance level has been violated on the upside, subsequent declines will find support there. Thus, resistance levels once violated reverse their role to support.

Once this resistance has been overcome, the natural place to look for a bottom will be at the former place of resistance. Yes, you guessed it...at (A) in Figure 3.4.

Figure 3.3 Support/Resistance Reversal Role

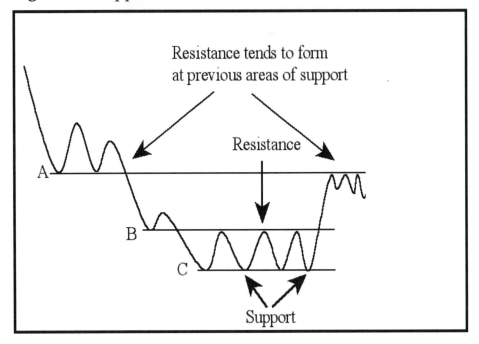

Figure 3.4 Resistance/Support Reversal Role

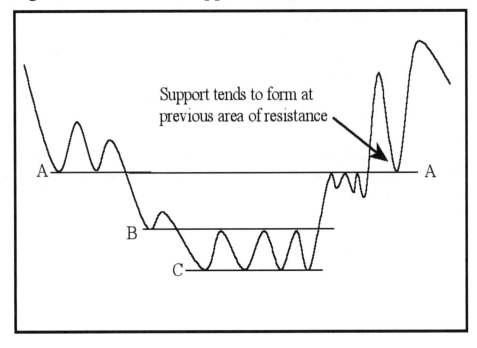

How to Determine the Significance of Support and Resistance Areas

There are several rules for determining the significance of any support or resistance area, but the three most important are:

1. The more times a zone has been able to halt or reverse a price trend, the greater its significance.

This is perhaps the most important rule. If the price keeps bouncing off a support level, people get used to the idea. Then, when it is finally breached, those who have become accustomed to buying there and selling at a profit are forced to sell at a loss. Others would have placed stop losses below the support level. The longer it is established the more obvious it becomes that this is the level to place stops. As the support gives way confidence is lost until a new level at a lower price is established. The same principle, in reverse, works for a resistance zone.

2. The steeper the price move preceding a given support or resistance zone, the greater its significance.

Think of trying to lift a heavy weight. If you make the attempt after running a fast race, you are less likely to succeed than someone who has not had to make such a dash. Markets are the same way. A modest support or resistance barrier is likely to be much more significant if prices have been racing ahead or declining sharply than if the price has been experiencing a slow, steady advance or decline.

3. The more a security changes hands at a particular level, the more <u>significant</u> that level is likely to be as a support/ resistance zone.

People tend to remember their own experiences. This means that the larger the number of people who have bought, or sold, at a particular level, the greater the significance the level will have as a potential support/resistance zone. If a lot of participants bought at $8 and the price declines to $6, there will be a rush of sell orders at $8 when the price rallies. This is because people have a problem taking losses, but are far more comfortable with breaking even.

Summary

1. A support area is a concentration of demand, sufficient to halt a decline, at least temporarily.

2. A resistance area is a concentration of supply, sufficient to turn back an advance, at least temporarily.

3. Once violated, a support zone reverses its role to resistance on the way back up and resistance reverses its role to support on the way down.

4. Once penetrated, a resistance zone reverses its role to one of support on the way down.

5. Support and resistance zones gain significance from the number of times they have successfully turned back a trend, the amount of volume that has been transacted at that level, and the greater the speed of the preceding price movement.

Support and Resistance Examples, Part I

Now it is time to take a look at a few charts. Chart 3.1 features a 15-minute bar of Wal-Mart. The price sank to a low, just above $79, early on Monday morning. Lows and highs are useful because they often become support and resistance areas. In this case, we would expect the low to become a possible buying area in the event that the price comes back to $79. As you can see, this was certainly the case during the first hour of Tuesday's trading (A). The next decline is halted on Wednesday morning (B), but this time the price gaps right through the support at Thursday's opening (C). The price does not decline back to $79, but is held at what was formerly resistance in a congestion area. You can also see that the Wednesday/Thursday gap was closed late on Thursday morning (D). This is normal since most gaps are eventually filled. As soon as that happens, another gap is opened up on Friday morning (D). See how Wednesday's rally high, which was resistance, now reverses its role. The gap also provides some support. Gaps, in and of themselves, often represent pivotal points and the downside gap between Tuesday and Wednesday halts Friday morning's rally (E). The price then falls through support at $80 (F) and finds a bottom at the lower end of the Thursday morning trading range. The easy penetration of the $80 area shows that support and resistance zones are intelligent places where the probabilities favor a turnaround, but they certainly do not guarantee one. The savvy trader will be on the lookout for other factors, such as oversold conditions in momentum indicators, the presence of moving averages and trendlines, etc., since these will increase the probabilities that the support or resistance zone will hold prices again. The price gaps up again on Tuesday morning (G) and is quickly filled within the hour. However, this decline is briefly held this time at $80. Just because a support/resistance area does not act as a pivotal point does not mean that it has lost its powers to do so in the future.

The price then continues up and is held at the resistance marked by the closing of the Wednesday morning gap (H), but this is only temporary since a nice extension to the rally develops once the resistance has been overcome.

Support and Resistance Examples, Part II

Quite often support and resistance areas develop around round numbers. This is because players have a habit of using these as mental stop points to buy or sell. Chart 3.2 features a 7.5-minute bar for the S&P Composite. During Tuesday and Wednesday, the Index rallies from the low 1,200's but there are only two round number pivotal points, 1,240 and 1,260. I have marked the higher one (A) for closer examination. You can see that the price action also established additional minor support and resistance points, which are flagged with horizontal trendlines at (B), (C), and (D). These are all possible support points when the price finally reverses direction.

Chart 3.1 Wal-Mart Stores, Inc. 15-minute Bar

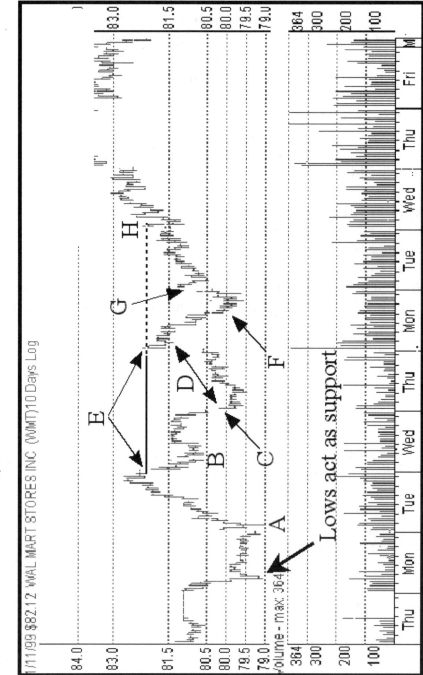

As time progresses into the Thursday opening, it is possible to appreciate that the round number 1,260 did turn out to be a support area. Also, you can see that the subsequent rally was turned back right at the Thursday morning gap (E). There are three places where we might expect to see the subsequent decline to hold: The level of the minor rally high (line A) in Chart 3.3, (line B) at the Wednesday minor high and Thursday and Friday minor lows, and, of course, the 1,260 area (line C). In the end, it was the round number 1,260 that proved to be the major support level. I may be stretching this a bit because the lower part of the bar was definitely below the 1,260 actual level. But, remember, with support and resistance levels we never know for sure where prices will turn. The key is to isolate the main ones. Then, when prices reach the general zone, look at the other indicators because this could be the place where the prevailing trend will possibly reverse.

Once it appears that the price has found support at 1,260 it is necessary to draw in the potential resistance points (Chart 3.4). This gives us a probable reversal point for subsequent rallies. As you can see, a couple of these lines did act as pivotal points for

Chart 3.2 S&P Composite 7.5-minute Bar

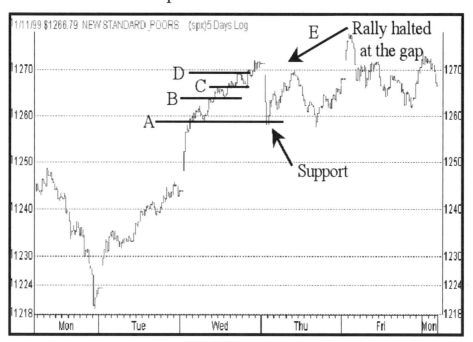

very minor rallies and reactions. Friday actually opens with a
gap right at the place where the market had experienced a previous gap (A), but notice what happens later. This same area of
gaps and resistance marked by the Wednesday close and the Friday opening just above 1,270 was instrumental in turning back
the mid-Friday and early Monday rallies (B).

Finally, in Chart 3.5, we turn to an example using a 7.5-minute
bar chart of Newmont Mining, a gold stock. Once again, it is important to look for temporary highs to mark potential support/
resistance areas for future price action. In this regard, we see a
high early on Tuesday morning (A). This could be expected to
form support in the event that the price rallies above this level
during the next advance. You can see that it took two attempts to
achieve this, since one bar just failed to break above the horizontal line. Then, on the reaction move from the breakout, the price
does find support at the extended (line B). As Wednesday opens
with a gap, the obvious potential zone of support lies at the Tuesday high at line (C). As you can see, the closing of the gap at
Tuesday's high once again acts as excellent support. I am refer-

Chart 3.3 S&P Composite 7.5-minute Bar

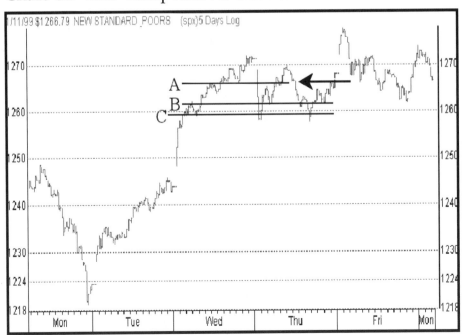

Chart 3.4 S&P Composite 7.5-minute Bar

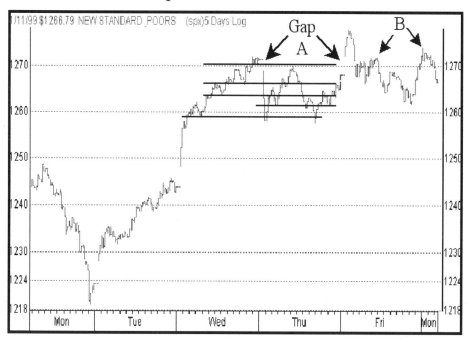

ring here to the gap against Wednesday's trading range, not the gap on the intraday chart; i.e., the distance between Tuesday's close and Wednesday's opening, because that is not closed. Resistance for the next rally could either be expected to come at the rally high, (A in Chart 3.6) or at the minor peak just below (B). The ellipse shows that volume was quite heavy at this point, so a lot of traders could well decide to take profits in the event the price rises to (B) again. And that is exactly what happened. The next decline is halted at our "gap/previous high support area" (C) once more. Then the price gaps up at (D) and the opening range acts as a support area (E) for the rest of the day. Later it zigzags higher, finding support at the close on Monday at (F); i.e., at Thursday's and Friday's minor rally highs.

Tuesday's opening, in Chart 3.7, gaps down at (A). We might have expected the price to find support at the middle trendline, but instead it declines all the way to the gap-closing attempt on Thursday. Note how the early Tuesday rally finds resistance at the middle line.

Chart 3.5 Newmont Mining 7.5-minute Bar

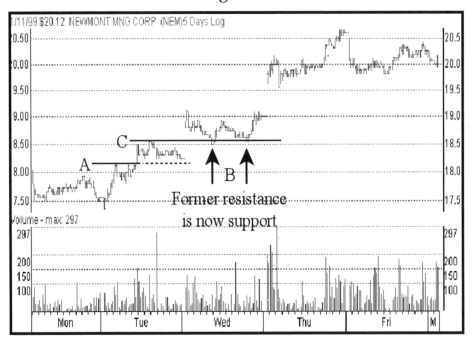

I could give you many more examples, but there are four points that really should be emphasized:

1. Peaks and troughs are continually reversing themselves as they alternate between support and resistance areas (peaks and troughs are continually reversing their support/resistance roles).

2. The upper and lower areas of gaps usually represent crucial pivotal points.

3. Support/resistance areas are not predictors of where prices will turn, but merely indicate possible or probable points.

4. Support/resistance analysis requires the intelligent inclusion of other indicators upon which a consensus of probabilities is arrived. ■

Chart 3.6 Newmont Mining 7.5-minute Bar

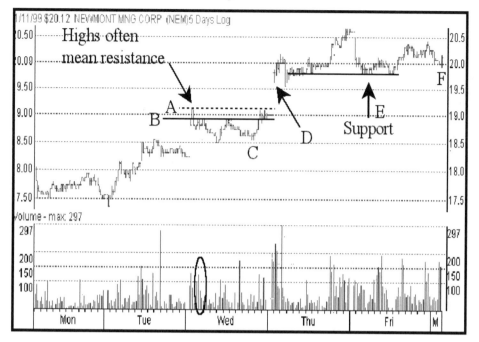

Chart 3.7 Newmont Mining 7.5-minute Bar

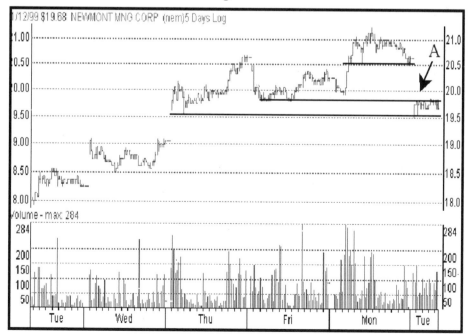

Chapter 4

Trendlines

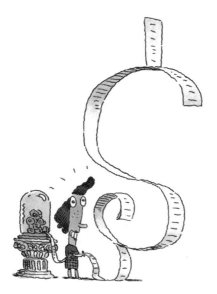

The Basics

In **technical analysis**, we are concerned with identifying a reversal in the price trend at an early stage and riding on the trend until the weight of the evidence proves that the trend has once again reversed. **Trendlines** represent one of these pieces of evidence, and, I might add, normally one of the strongest and most reliable. They are probably the simplest of all technical tools, but do not let the simplicity fool you—trendlines are also one of the most effective. A **down trendline** is constructed by joining a series of declining peaks as in Figure 4.1. It is normal to begin with the first or highest peak and then connect the line to the second one. The line is then extended, and when the price breaks above the line, a buy signal is triggered.

Never draw a line that only touches one of the peaks because it is not valid; correctly drawn trendlines should reflect the underlying trend. In Figure 4.2, the line is arbitrarily drawn through space and does not have any significance, whatsoever, when penetrated.

Figure 4.1 Down Trendline

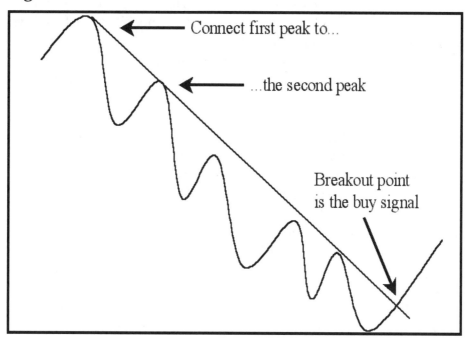

Figure 4.2 Down Trendline

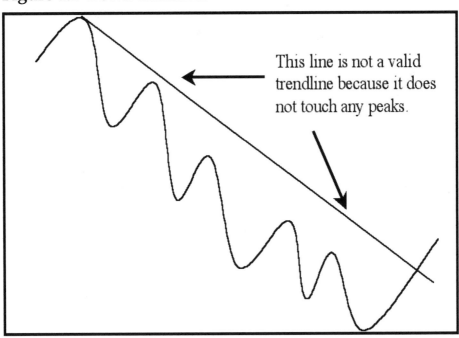

This line is not a valid
trendline because it does
not touch any peaks.

An **up trendline** is constructed in an advancing market, as shown in Figure 4.3, by connecting a series of bottoms. It is normal to begin the line at the final low and connect it to the first low. When the price eventually falls below the line, a sell signal is triggered. Once again, never draw a trendline that does not touch more than two bottoms (Figure 4.4) because it will be meaningless when penetrated.

Sometimes, as in Figure 4.5, the price rises so quickly that when a line joins the ultimate low and the first bottom, it results in an extremely sharp angle of ascent. This is not of much use since the steepness of the line renders the trend unsustainable.

Remember, a good trendline should reflect the underlying trend, and this one does not. It would be far better to draw a line like the longer one in Figure 4.5 that joins more bottoms and has a smaller, but more sustainable, angle of ascent. The same principles of common sense trendline construction would be applied in reverse or a down trendline.

The line in Figure 4.6 was briefly penetrated in the ellipse. You may be asking why that did not qualify as a sell signal? The an-

Figure 4.3 Up Trendline

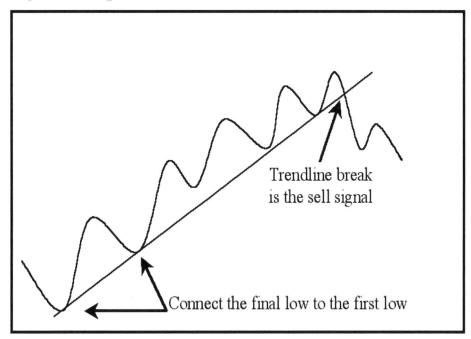

Figure 4.4 Up Trendline

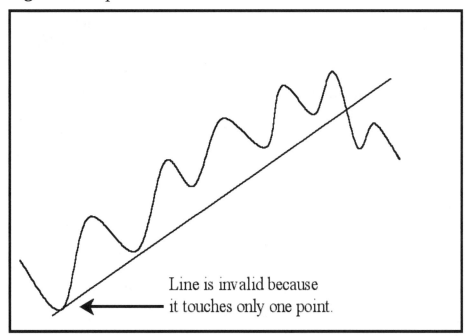

Figure 4.5 What to Connect?

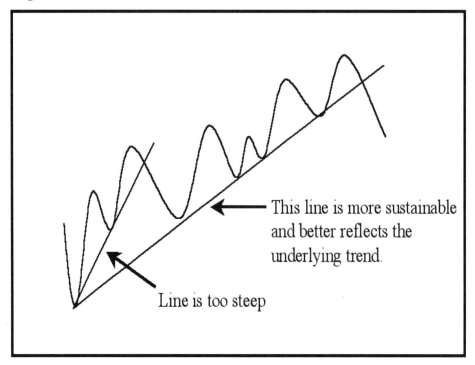

This line is more sustainable and better reflects the underlying trend.

Line is too steep

swer is a penetration must be decisive before it can qualify. You need to give the price a little wiggle room before pronouncing the prevailing trend dead. Unfortunately, what constitutes a decisive penetration is a matter of judgment, common sense, and experience.

When an up trendline is decisively penetrated, one of two things occur: Either the trend break signals an actual reversal in trend, as we see in Figure 4.7, or the trend changes from up to sideways as in Figure 4.8. This is known as a **consolidation break**. In this case, the trendline penetration signals a temporary pause before higher prices are seen.

The same alternatives apply when a down trendline is violated. The trend is either reversed, as in Figure 4.9, or the break slows the downside momentum as the trend changes from down to sideways (Figure 4.10). In this instance, the sideways trading range eventually gives way to an actual trend reversal. You can now appreciate that trendlines can be horizontal, as well as up or down, because the horizontal lines also join peaks and troughs.

Figure 4.6 What is a Valid Penetration?

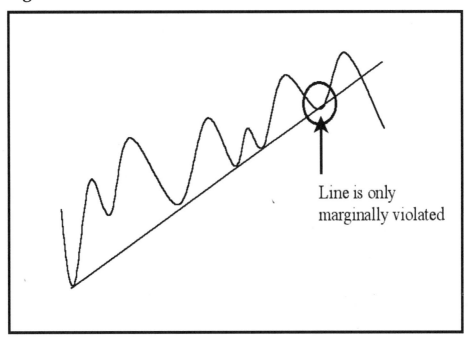

Figure 4.7 Implications of a Trendline Break

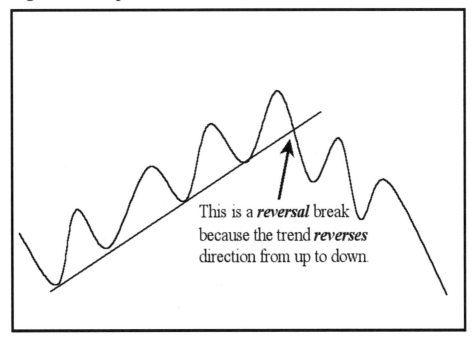

Figure 4.8 Implications of a Trendline Break

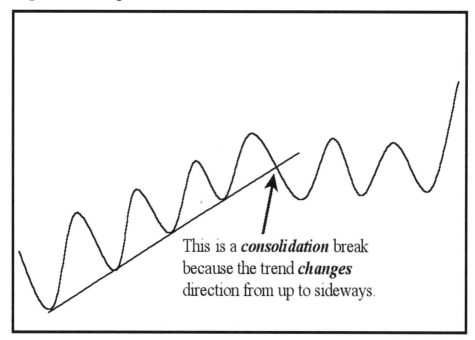

This is a ***consolidation*** break because the trend ***changes*** direction from up to sideways.

Figure 4.9 Implications of a Trendline Break

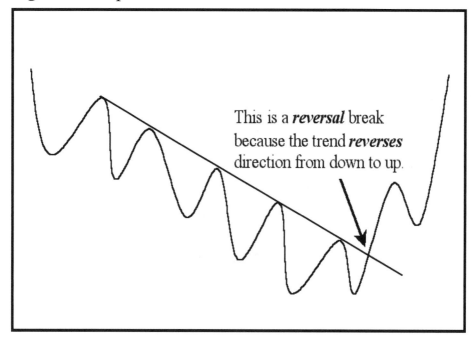

This is a ***reversal*** break because the trend ***reverses*** direction from down to up.

Summary

1. Down trendlines connect peaks; up trendlines connect bottoms.

2. Trendlines are not valid when they touch one or less points.

3. Trendlines should reflect the underlying trend.

4. Trendlines should be decisive.

5. Trendline violations signal both reversals and consolidations.

Figure 4.10 Implications of a Trendline Break

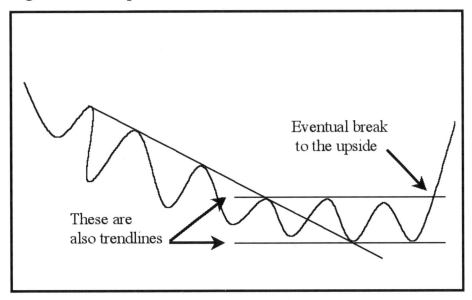

Establishing the Significance of a Trendline

Before we take a look at some actual marketplace examples, I would like to explain the three rules for determining the importance of an individual line:

1. A trendline reflects the underlying trend: the longer the line, other things being equal, the greater the significance of its penetration.

2. A good trendline is really a dynamic area of support on the way up, or resistance on the way down. The more times a line has been touched or approached, the greater its significance as a support or resistance zone; therefore, the stronger the signal when the line is finally penetrated.

3. The steeper the angle of ascent or descent, the less sustainable the trend; therefore, the less significant will be the penetration.

Marketplace Examples

Chart 4.1 features a closing chart based on 30-minute bars for the S&P Composite. It is possible to use the actual bars themselves because this has the advantage of normally giving earlier signals. However, bar charts also come with two disadvantages. The first is that while timeliness means quicker signals it also involves the penalty of more whipsaws. Second, if you are not spending your entire time trading, or if you are trading several different entities simultaneously, it is far easier to pick closing points and set stops ahead of time than it is with bar charts.

In this instance, the price starts off in an uptrend and we are able to construct an up trendline (A). Line (A) represents our stop level. To ensure that any violations have a better chance of being valid, the stop would be placed a bit below the line, and, of course, is raised progressively as the price works its way higher. This

Chart 4.1 S&P Composite

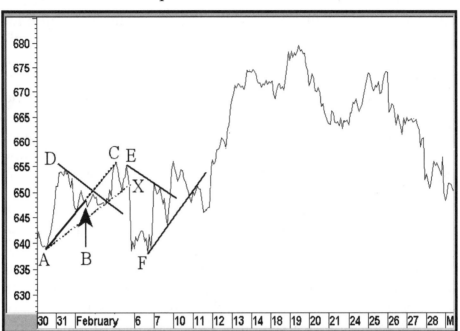

trend continues for a while, but the price soon falls below the line, and the position is stopped out (B). As time progresses, you can see the next rally is halted at the extended line (C). This is an important point because it is a rule of trendline analysis: once penetrated, a trendline reverses its support/resistance role. For example, if an up trendline is violated, the extended line becomes one of resistance, and vice versa. In this case, the greater the significance of the line prior to its penetration, the greater its significance as a support/resistance area. We can actually draw a line (C) joining the two little peaks and use its violation as a buy signal. The stop would then be placed below dashed trendline (A). This new trendline, which is drawn with a slower angle of ascent, is violated fairly soon for a small profit, but there is no down trendline that can be constructed for stop purposes in the event we decide to go short. In a situation like this, it is either better to go flat or alternatively go short, but place the stop above the previous high. This decision should be made on the basis of what the risk would be; i.e., the difference between the penetration and the high—if it seems too great, then don't do it. After all, there will always be another opportunity. In a real life situation, you would also take a look at what the consensus of other indicators, such as momentum or oscillators, are flashing. I will have more to say on this a little later on.

Once a rally has taken place and a decline set in, we are in a position to construct another trendline (E). Initially this looks like a very profitable trade as the price rallies to the old high around 655. We can also construct an up trendline (F) for stop purposes. This is just as well, since the price soon whips its way back down again and a small loss is taken. Had we used the E down trendline as the stop, the loss would have been even greater since this line is declining.

We can now draw another down trendline (A) (Chart 4.2) and it is soon violated with a violent rally. An up trendline for stop purposes can be constructed at point (F), but only an hour after the rally starts the price is well away from the line. This means that a lot of profits would have to be given up in the event of a quick reversal. In such cases the best technique is to use a momentum indicator as a signaling device to take at least partial

Chart 4.1   S&P Composite (Repeated)

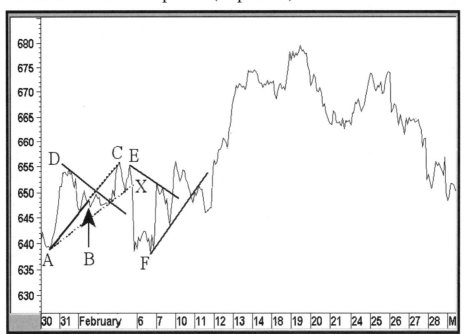

profits. This approach is discussed at length in Chapter 9. Once
the next decline gets underway and a small bottom is established,
it is then possible to construct a less steep trendline (C) and use its
penetration as a stop loss point. Also, it is possible to draw another small down trendline joining two little peaks (B) as a basis
for a purchase. This trade leads to a small profit before our new
(C) trendline is violated.

Anyone going short on the violation of (C) would have made
a good profit. However, because the decline was so steep, there
was no opportunity to construct a down trendline, which could
be used as a basis for placing a stop. The high for the move at (D)
would, once again, have to be the benchmark for a stop, and an
oversold oscillator as a flashing point for taking at least partial
profits.

Now if we replot the shallow trendline (E) from Chart 4.2 into
Chart 4.3 you can see that it was eventually violated at point (X).
The horizontal and vertical connecting arrows show that a profit
was achieved. However, this was less than the profit achieved
from the steeper (C) line. Note how this extended line reversed

Chart 4.2 S&P Composite

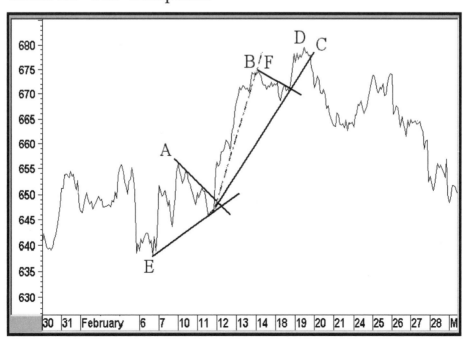

its role from support to resistance once it had been violated (Chart 4.4).

The next buy signal (Chart 4.5) came from the penetration of a small down trendline (B3). This does not look like a very impressive line and, indeed, it is not since it is short and has not been touched or approached very often. However, we should not forget that a good trendline reflects the underlying trend. It is possible to extend the line back to (A), and you can see that this "new" line is really an extension of a small down trendline we used as a buy signal. Thus, even though the line has been penetrated on both the upside and downside, it still retains some degree of importance when violated again.

Eventually, in Chart 4.6, you can see the rally developing. It is quite a sharp one because it takes the price above our long up trendline (in the left hand side of the circle). In effect, by rallying above this line, the price has moved above resistance because the extended line (D) reversed its role from support to resistance. We are now rolling the dice somewhat because the penetration of the line can mean one of two things. First, if the violation is valid and

Chart 4.3   S&P Composite

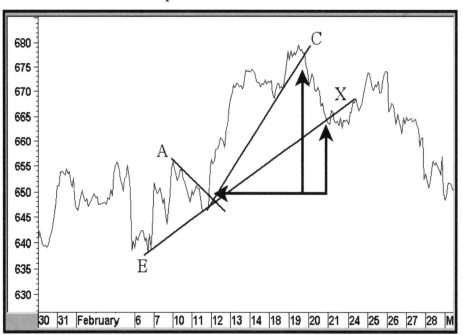

Chart 4.4 S&P Composite

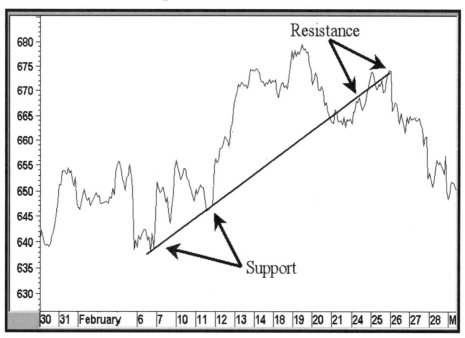

Chart 4.5 S&P Composite

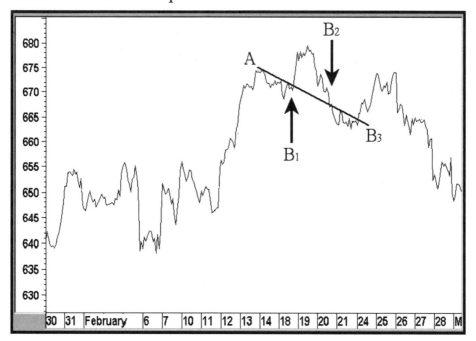

the price continues to rally, it indicates the uptrend will take place at a faster rate. Second, if the price cannot stay above the line, it will represent an exhaustion move and that will be equally as significant, but this time on the bearish side.

In this case the price fails to hold above the line. It even tries again to rally above it, but is unable to experience a decisive penetration as signaled in the ellipse. We are then able to construct another small up trendline (Chart 4.7), and the price breaks below both lines for a double break. The price then declines. This makes it possible to draw the small down trendline (A) in Chart 4.8 as a stop point for covering or going long. However, the exhaustion move above the trendline (circled area on Chart 4.6), that took place earlier, combined with the double break, results in further downside action since the technical position is very weak indeed. After a small rally, it is then possible to draw a steeper line (B), but it is never meaningfully penetrated.

Next, on Chart 4.9, there is a quick 30-minute advance that does move marginally above the line at (X). It is arguable that a purchase, or the covering of a short position could have been made

Chart 4.6 S&P Composite

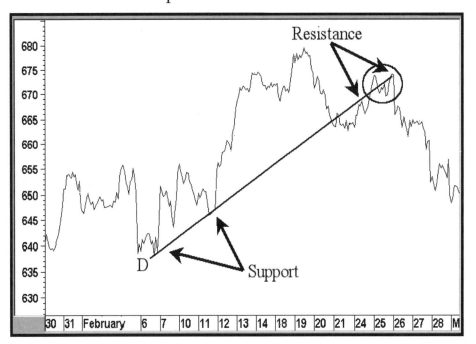

Chart 4.7   S&P Composite

Chart 4.8   S&P Composite

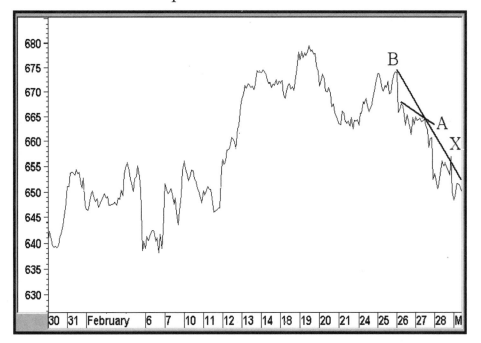

at that point. Once the price moved back below the line, though, any long positions should immediately be stopped out for two reasons. First, the price fell below the line, thereby canceling out the justification for the purchase in the first place. Second, and perhaps more important, the temporary penetration represented an exhaustion move which typically signals above average technical weakness.

Return Line Breakouts

Several points in the example above should be explained further. These relate to the penetration of resistance lines in an uptrend and support lines in a downtrend. Up to now we have assumed that the only trendline we could construct is an uptrend one that joins the lows. However, in some cases it is also possible to construct a line connecting a series of highs. This is known as a **return line**. The question then arises as to what follows in the event that these trendlines are violated on the upside—a **positive**

Chart 4.9   S&P Composite

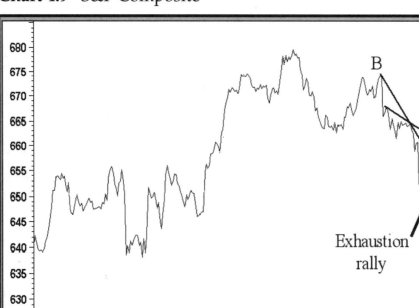

breakout. There are two possibilities. The first is that the penetration of the line represents a signal the uptrend will continue, but at a faster pace, as in Figure 4.11. The other develops when the penetration proves to be marginal, as in Figure 4.12, or very temporary, and the price then slips back below the line. This represents **exhaustion** and is a kind of sell signal because it indicates technical weakness. How do we know whether the penetration will be valid or not? The answer is we do not. There are some characteristics we can be on the lookout for, though. For example, if the trendline is very steep, the breakout is less likely to be sustainable. Therefore, the odds would favor exhaustion. On the other hand, if the line is less steep, then the breakout is more likely to represent a successful assault on a major resistance level. Figures 4.13 and 4.14 show that the same return line principles apply in reverse for down trendlines. In Figure 4.13, a penetration of a steep line is likely to represent exhaustion. The penetration, or a **negative breakout** of a less steep line, represents a signal of a decline picking up downside momentum (Figure 4.14). In this case, the line is constructed by joining a series of bottoms. ∎

Figure 4.11 Positive Breakout

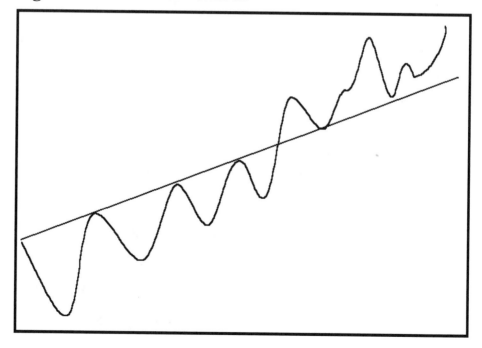

Figure 4.12 Exhaustion

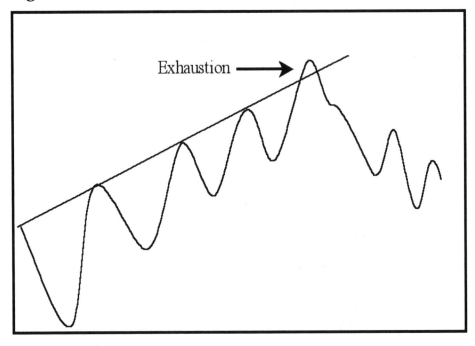

Figure 4.13 Exhaustion

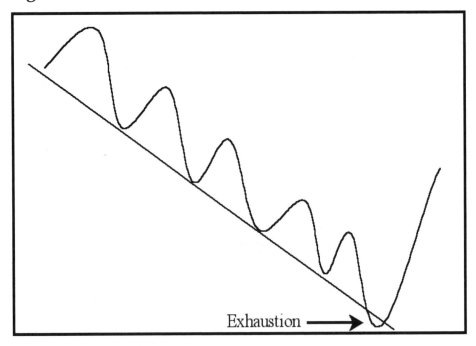

Figure 4.14 Negative Breakout Indicates
Greater Downside Momentum

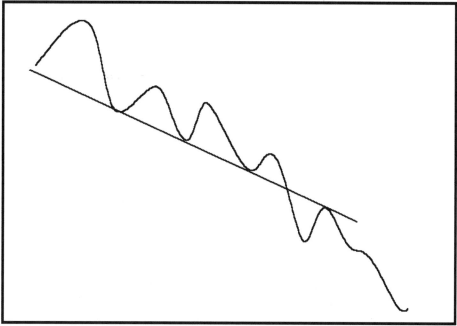

Chapter 5

Price Pattern
Formations

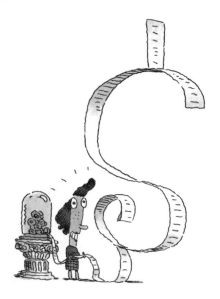

Introduction

If you look at a chart of any freely traded market, you will rarely find that it reverses on a dime, as in Figure 5.1. Normally, the uptrend is separated from the downtrend by some ranging action as in the left part of Figure 5.2. The same is true of a reversal from down to up in the right part of that figure. Over the years, technicians have observed that these trading ranges take on certain characteristics, which are known as **price patterns** or **price formations**.

Rectangles

In Figure 5.3, the price starts off in an uptrend. Eventually, upside momentum dissipates and it experiences some kind of a trading range. Every time it falls to the lower level, buyers are

Figure 5.1 The Holy Grail Market

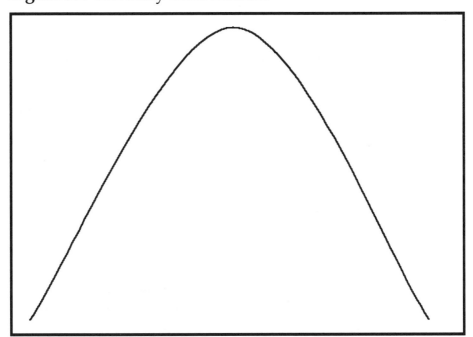

Figure 5.2 Trading Ranges

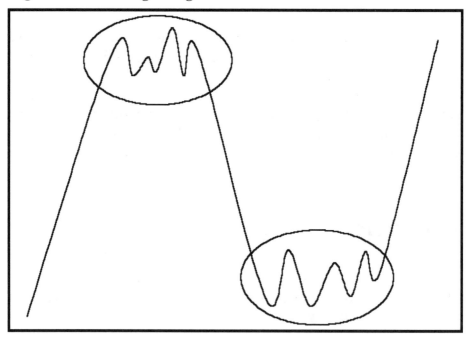

attracted and sellers are less enthusiastic. As the price rises to the upper end of the range, it is the *sellers* who are more enthusiastic and *buyers* who pull back.

Many times a trendline can be drawn connecting the peaks and another connecting the bottoms. This makes it possible to see that the battle between buyers and sellers has two demarcation lines. Imagine some trench warfare going on. Army A and Army B are continually battling between themselves, but neither is able to cross through enemy lines. Eventually, one side wins out and the other is forced to pull back. Well, the same type of concept is apparent in the charts. Eventually buyers or sellers will gain control. In this case, it is the sellers who win, and the break is below the lower trendline, indicating the uptrend has now been reversed and a downtrend is now in force. This trading range is a pattern that is known as a **rectangle**. In this case, it is a reversal pattern because the rectangle reversed the bullish-bias of buyers to a bearish-bias favoring the sellers. **Reversal patterns** at market tops are known as **distribution** and at market bottoms as **accumulation**. The concept is that the security is moving or being distributed

Figure 5.3 Rectangle Formation

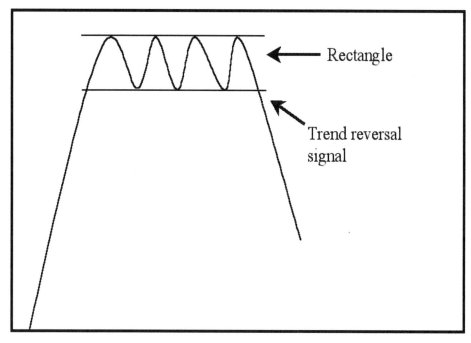

from strong to weak hands at tops. At bottoms, smart money is said to be accumulating the security in question. Had the battle been resolved in favor of the buyers, the rectangle would have represented a temporary pause or consolidation in the uptrend. In this instance the pattern or formation would have been termed a **continuation** or **consolidation rectangle** as in Figure 5.4.

In technical analysis, it is said that a trend is a trend is a trend. What this means is that it is always assumed that the existing trend is in force until evidence to the contrary evolves. In *this* case, the evidence to the contrary evolved when the rectangle broke to the downside, but until that point the uptrend was still considered to be in force. Rectangles, as with most price patterns, come with measuring objectives. Figure 5.5 shows that you would measure the maximum distance between the high and the low of the pattern *and* project the distance down. This is said to be the **minimum ultimate downside objective**. The term "minimum" is used because prices often move much more than indicated. Ultimate means that the objective may not be achieved in one move, but could take several rallies and reactions before it reaches its goal.

Figure 5.4 Continuation, or Consolidation Rectangle

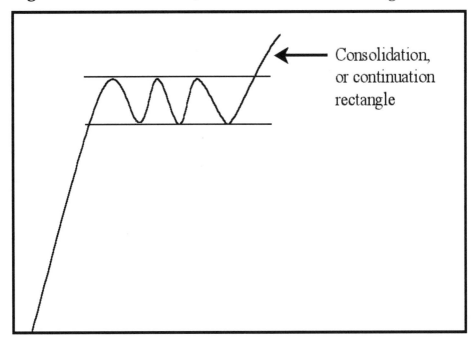

Figure 5.5 Minimum Ultimate Measuring Objective

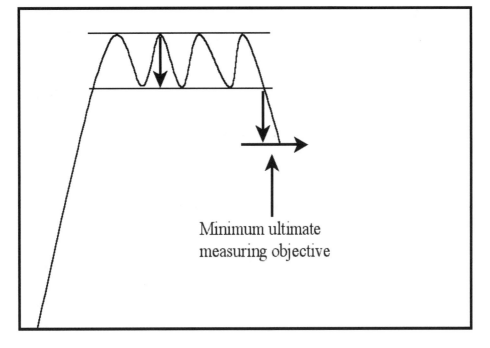

In Figure 5.6 we see a breakout from a rectangle that separates a downtrend from an uptrend. After the breakout, the price experiences a pull back towards the pattern. This is known as a **retracement move**. After the retracement, it then goes on to reach the objective. Retracement moves can be frustrating, since they occur quite often, but the good news is that they offer traders a second chance to buy.

Volume considerations are important in pattern formation and breakouts. It is normal, when a rectangle is being formed, for the trend of volume to shrink as in Chart 5.1. During an upside breakout it is imperative for volume to expand noticeably; otherwise the breakout is suspect. For downside breakouts, the volume configuration is unimportant, although expanding volume is usually more bearish.

Another important characteristic is the size or the length taken to complete a pattern. The logic for this is fairly obvious; a pattern represents a place where buyers and sellers are at battle with each other. The longer the battle takes the more significant the victory and, therefore, the longer the ensuing trend. A military analogy

Figure 5.6 Retracement Move

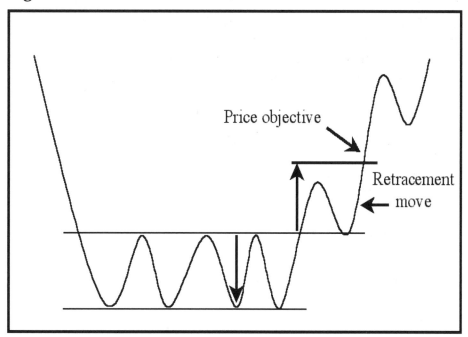

Chart 5.1 Newmont Mining

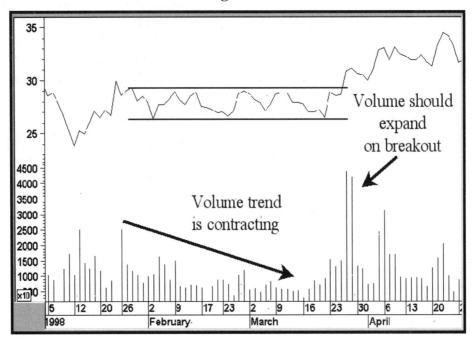

might involve a fight between two patrols. When either wins, the other side experiences a setback, but when the whole army beats the other, an actual war is won or lost. The implication of winning a war is far greater than beating a single patrol.

Intraday charts contain small patterns in comparison to weekly or monthly charts, so the implications are far less significant. In the same way, a pattern completed by a tick chart will be far less significant than one completed using hourly bars.

Rectangles are just one of many chart patterns. There is not enough time in this book to cover them all, but I would like to describe several that appear more commonly in intraday charts.

Head and Shoulders

Perhaps the most notorious is the **head and shoulders** (Figure 5.7). This formation appears at both bottoms and tops. At tops, it consists of a final rally separated by two smaller ones. The line connecting the lows is called the **neckline** and the **measuring objective** is obtained by calculating the distance from the head to the neckline and then projecting that measuring objective down. Head and shoulders can contain horizontal lines, as shown in this example. In this instance, when the price violates the neckline, it also breaks below the previous low. In effect, the head and shoulders completion signals that a series of declining peaks and troughs is now in force. Alternatively, (Figure 5.8), the line can slope up. This formation is known as an **upward sloping head and shoulders**. Conversely, when the neckline is in a declining mode, (Figure 5.9), it is called a **downward sloping head and shoulders**.

Reverse head and shoulders (or head and shoulders bottoms) form after a decline (Figure 5.10). They, too, have the usual measuring implications and come in the upward and downward sloping variety.

Figure 5.7 Head and Shoulders Pattern

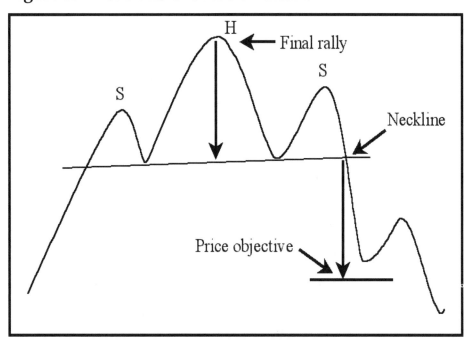

Figure 5.8 Upward Sloping Head and Shoulders Pattern

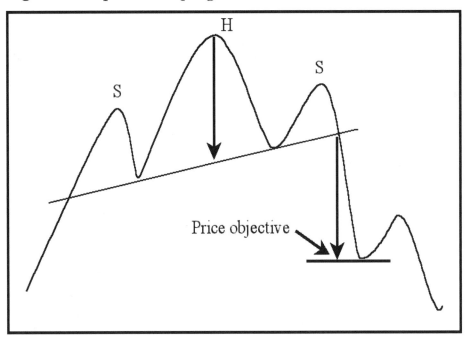

Figure 5.9 Downward Sloping Head and Shoulders Pattern

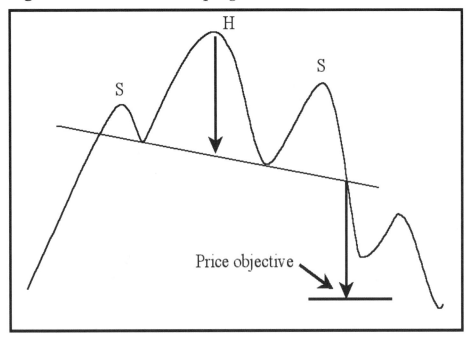

Head and Shoulder Failures

Sometimes a head and shoulders pattern appears to be forming, but instead of breaking down, the price rallies from the neckline (Figure 5.11), subsequently making a new high for the move. Also, it may first break down and then reverse as in Figure 5.12. Such situations are known as **head and shoulders failures** and are usually quite bullish. The big question is how do you know when it has broken down? There is no black and white answer; we can only deal in shades of gray on this one. The first indication of a possible failure comes when the price rallies above the down trendline joining the head and the right shoulder as in Figure 5.12. In this instance, the shallower the line, the greater the significance of the break. Line (X) is quite steep, so I would not place as much significance on the break as I would on line (B) in Figure 5.11, which is much shallower. The second, and perhaps balance tipping point, is when the price rallies above the right shoulder (Figure 5.13). At this juncture, we now have a series of

Figure 5.10 Reverse Head and Shoulders Pattern

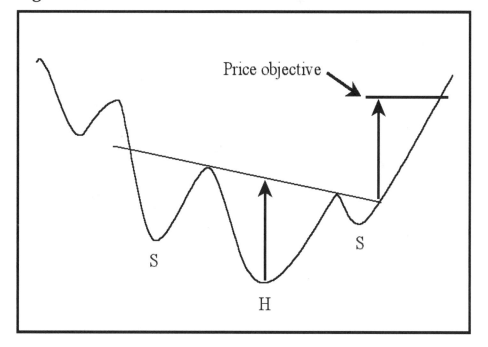

Figure 5.11 Head and Shoulders Failure

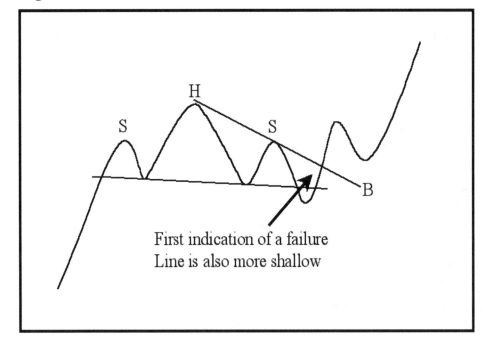

Figure 5.12 Head and Shoulders Failure

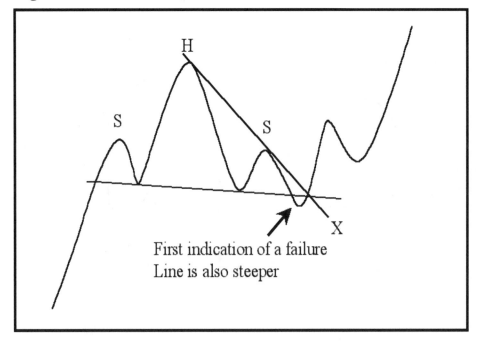

rising peaks. If the neckline has not been violated on a horizontal head and shoulders, it means the series of rising bottoms that presumably preceded the formation of the head and shoulders is still intact. Therefore, the trend, as defined by peak and trough analysis, is still bullish. The final signal, which is more of a confirmation, is when the price rallies above the head. In terms of market action, the rally above the right shoulder is usually the best place to enter a buy signal because you can place a good, reasonably low risk stop below the neckline. The same principle holds for an **inverse head and shoulders**, but in reverse.

Triangles

Another common formation is the triangle. A triangle is constructed from two converging trendlines, one joining a series of peaks and another a series of troughs. Breakouts develop when the price violates either of these lines. In Figure 5.14 we see a down-

Figure 5.13 Head and Shoulders Failure

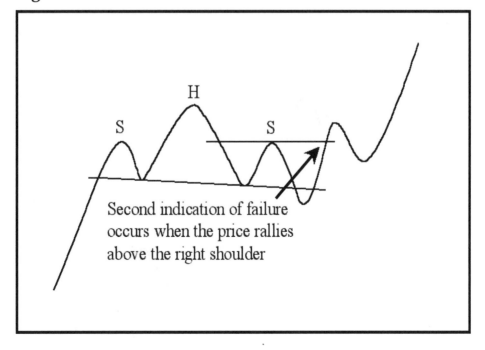

side breakout. When one line is declining and the other rising, the pattern is termed a **symmetrical triangle**. However, when one of the lines is horizontal it is known as a **right-angled triangle** (Figure 5.15). When a right-angled triangle contains a declining trendline it is generally a bearish pattern and is known as a **descending right-angled triangle**. The opposite, an **ascending right-angled triangle**, is generally bullish (Figure 5.16). The horizontal lines in these formations provide clearly definable support and resistance areas. Breakouts from right-angled triangles are usually more powerful than those from symmetrical ones. Triangles, like other patterns, can be of the reversal or continuation variety. Breakouts can sometimes be less reliable than with other patterns because what starts out as a right-angled triangle can sometimes turn into a rectangle.

Perhaps the most dynamic moves emanating from triangles develop when a right-angled variety breaks in the opposite direction to that expected. In Figure 5.17 the price does not break below the horizontal line of support, but in turn, rallies above the declining line. Figure 5.18 shows a breakout developing below a

Figure 5.14 Symmetrical Triangle

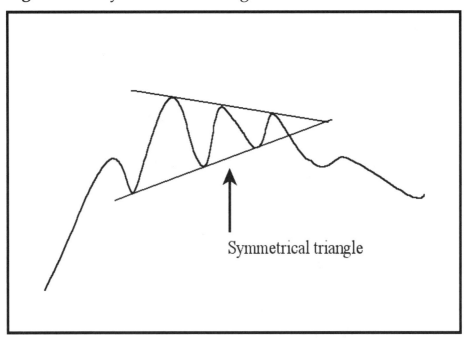

Symmetrical triangle

Figure 5.15 Descending Right Angle Triangle

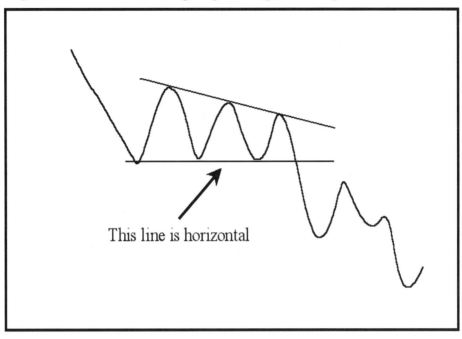

This line is horizontal

Figure 5.16 Ascending Right Angle Triangle

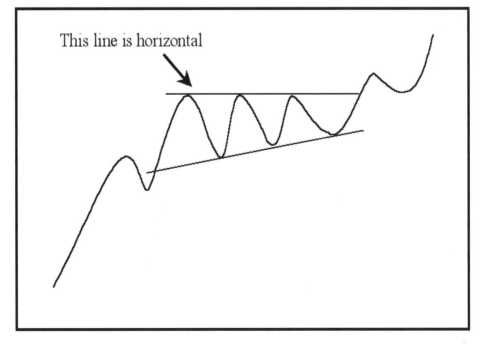

This line is horizontal

rising trendline. Nasty declines often follow from such breakouts, probably because the failure to rally above the horizontal level of resistance leads to exhaustion.

Double Bottoms and Tops

A **double top** develops in an uptrend and is a reversal pattern. After a rally and reaction, the subsequent advance fails to take the price meaningfully above the previous rally. It then retreats below the previous low and a reversal in trend is signaled (Figure 5.19). It does not really matter where the second top develops. Sometimes it is a little bit above the first, sometimes a bit below and occasionally at the same level. However, if the second peak tops out well above its predecessor, this does not count. What we are really seeing in this formation is a reversal in the rising peaks and troughs if we allow for the fact that the second peak is not significantly above the first.

Figure 5.17 Triangle

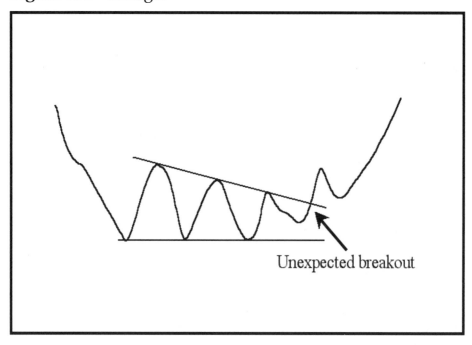

Figure 5.18 Triangle

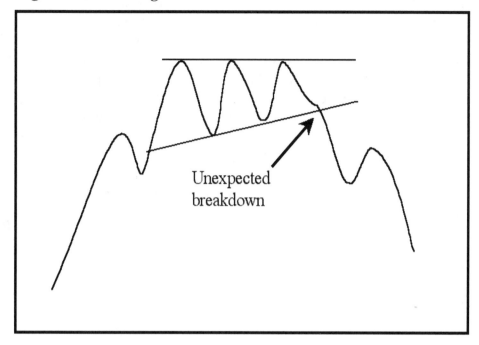

Figure 5.19 Double Tops

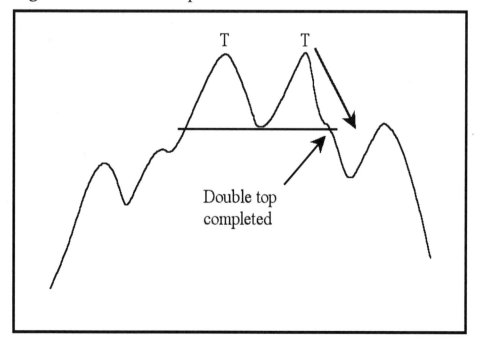

A **double bottom** (Figure 5.20) is exactly the opposite of a double top in that two reactions develop at around the same level, but the rally that forms after the formation of the second bottom takes the price above the previous peak. Both the first top and the first bottom in such formations are usually heavy volume, high excitement affairs. The second top and bottom are typically associated with far less volume and far less excitement. The mood on the second bottom is usually more bearish than at the first due to the disappointment that the rally off the first bottom is all but retraced. These patterns only appear on the charts as reversals, not continuation. The measuring objective is again taken by measuring the depth of the pattern and projecting it in the direction of the breakout.

Figure 5.20 Double Bottoms

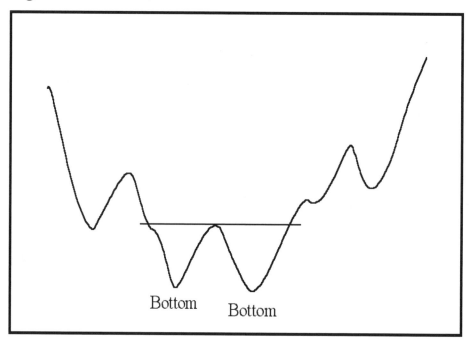

Summary

1. Uptrends and downtrends are normally separated by a trading range, which often takes the form of a recognizable price pattern.

2. Price patterns are either reversal, or continuation formations.

3. Reversal patterns at market peaks are known as distribution, and at market bottoms as accumulation.

4. Patterns offer price objectives when completed. These objectives are often exceeded.

Price Patterns in the Marketplace

Now it is time to put the diagrams away and look at some actual marketplace examples. One thing that is important to understand is the time frame of the chart in question. Comparing a 30-minute close to a tick chart can display substantially different information. This means that you need to explore several different time frames when considering chart formations. For example, Chart 5.2 shows a 15-minute close of the NYSE Composite. Not much to report here except to say that there was a declining trend that bottomed out on the opening of the 28th. Chart 5.3, though, is a tick for the NYSE Composite for the same period. Several chart formations are apparent. The actual bottom was in fact a double bottom formation. The first developed from a right-angled triangle.

Beginning at the upper left, the downtrend was preceded by a head and shoulders top formation. In this case the downside objective was more than achieved. Then, during the decline, the price completed a continuation right-angled triangle. The rally on the 28th was also associated with a continuation pattern, only this time it was a rectangle. Finally, we see a small upward sloping head and shoulders top.

Chart 5.4 features a two-day head and shoulders top, followed by a **head and shoulders consolidation**. Chart 5.5 encompasses a little bit of the previous one. This time, the price forms an inverse,

Chart 5.2   NYSE Composite and a 15-minute Close

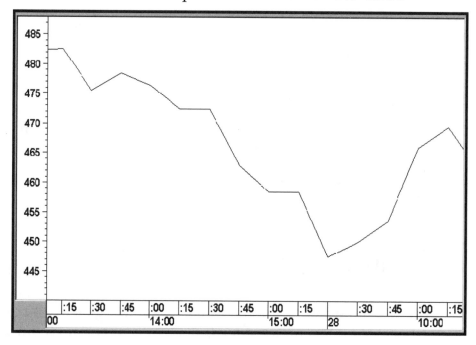

Chart 5.3   NYSE Composite Tick

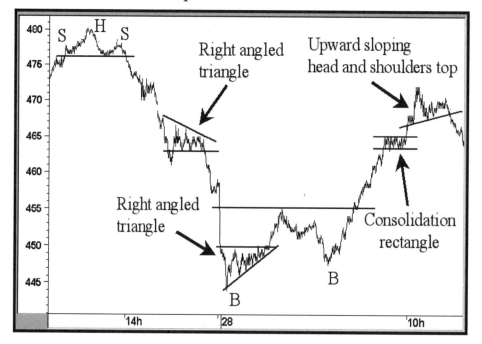

Chart 5.4 NYSE Composite 5-minute Bar

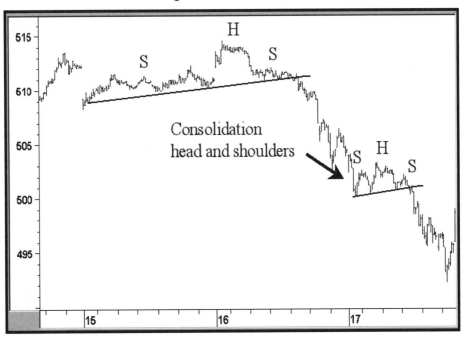

or reverse head and shoulders. This formation actually contains a couple of smaller patterns. First, you can see that the bottom of the head is really a reverse head and shoulders in its own right. After breaking out, the price then slipped below the neckline (A), offering the possibility that it might be a failure. However, it did not break below the right shoulder (Chart 5.6); so once the decline had run its course the rally continued. This pattern was different from the other examples since the breakout was followed by a **retracement move**. Retracements are quite common and actually give the trader a second chance to get in. They usually make easier entry points since breakouts typically develop in fast market conditions when emotions are running high and volume expands. On the other hand, volume shrinks and disinterest mounts during a retracement, thereby making this environment an easier place to make a purchase.

Chart 5.7 shows the same period, but now the bars have been increased to 30-minutes. The large reverse head and shoulders is still visible, but neither of the other two patterns—the consolidation head and shoulders contained in the upper ellipse, nor the

Chart 5.5 NYSE Composite 5-minute Bar

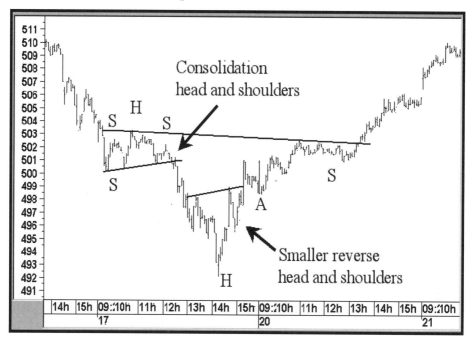

Chart 5.6 NYSE Composite 5-minute Bar

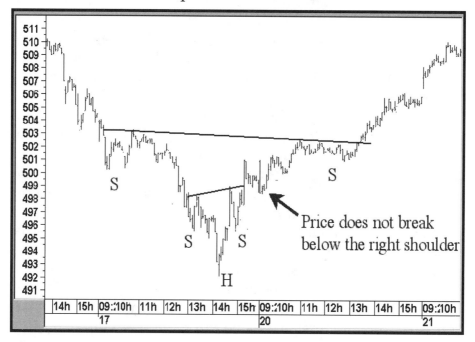

smaller reverse head and shoulders in the lower one—are evident. This shows that it is really important when trading some of the larger intraday time frames, such as 30 or 60 minutes, to also unravel some of the shorter ones to see what is going on under the surface.

One caveat to using extremely short time frames is that some markets are less liquid than others. In this respect, Chart 5.8 features a 1-minute bar chart of December 1997 gold. Clearly, there is not much to be gained by looking at such a short time frame. However, if the time frame is increased to 60 minutes, as in Chart 5.9, you can see that we get a much clearer picture of what is going on. For example, there is a rectangle and a good down trendline that can be constructed.

The 30-minute bar chart of December 1998 corn in Chart 5.10 looks as though it is in the process of forming a head and shoulders top. If this time frame is reduced as in Chart 5.11, to a 5-minute bar, the zigs and zags become much clearer. The minor support and resistance zones are also apparent. You can also see that the neckline was not violated, and the pattern eventually failed with

Chart 5.7 NYSE Composite 30-minute Bar

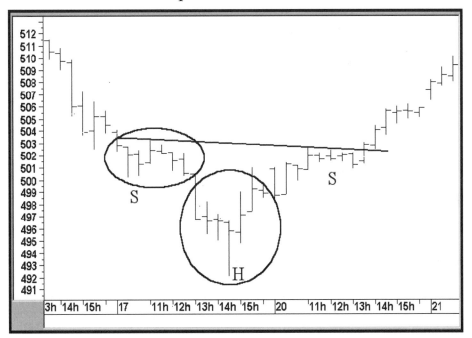

Chart 5.8   December 1997 Gold 1-minute Bar

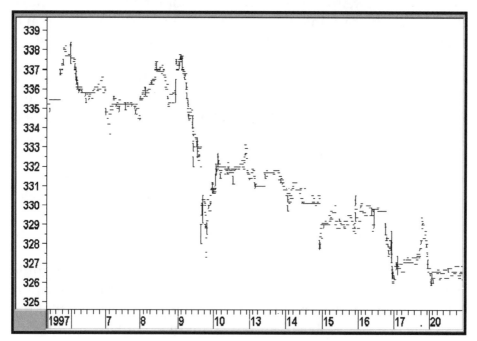

Chart 5.9   December 1997 Gold 60-minute Bar

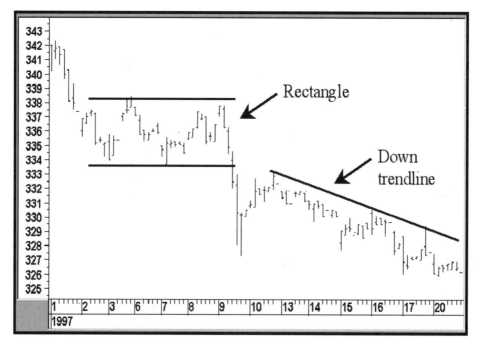

Chart 5.10 December 1998 Corn 30-minute Bar

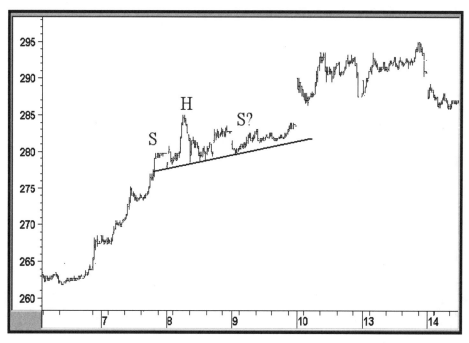

an explosive rally following. The odds began to favor a failure when the trendline joining the head with the two right shoulders was violated. Normally, it makes sense to wait for a break above the right shoulder, but this line had a fairly shallow angle of descent and had been touched several times. Chart 5.12 shows us that the right shoulders were really an ascending triangle. Here then, is an example of a situation that looked extremely bearish at the outset. Then the balance between buyers and sellers became very fine as volatility decreased. Once the buyers got the upper hand, they were able to run away with the ball. As the rally progressed (Chart 5.13), it looked as if the price was forming a consolidation reverse head and shoulders. Then an upside breakout materializes. This was the signal to buy. However, any profits soon turned to losses as the price reversed to the downside with a vengeance. The place to have liquidated was the final seconds of the day as the price fell below the lower part of the right shoulder. One would have had to be pretty quick because the next day's opening was much lower. Chart 5.13 also shows what happened a little later. After the price triggered the head and shoulders fail-

Chart 5.11 December 1998 Corn 5-minute Bar

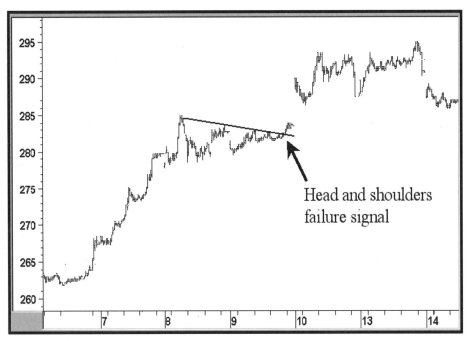

Head and shoulders
failure signal

Chart 5.12 December 1998 Corn 5-minute Bar

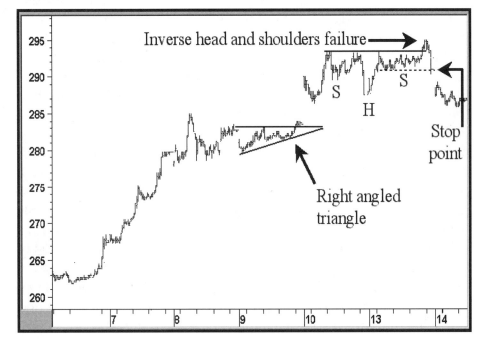

Inverse head and shoulders failure

S

H

S

Stop
point

Right angled
triangle

Chart 5.13 December 1998 Corn 5-minute Bar

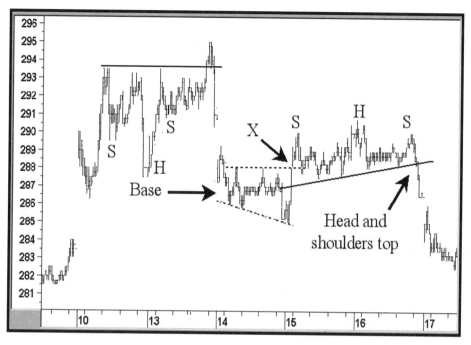

ure and dropped, it formed a base from which it broke out at the opening of the 15th (X). It looked as if a strong rally was underway, but the breakout was followed by a two day trading range. That trading range, if you look carefully, was actually a slightly upward sloping head and shoulders top. This demonstrates an important point: the **principle of cancellation**. Remember, the base, formed on the 14th, represents a battle between buyers and sellers, which the buyers won. From this point it is reasonable to expect the continued rout of sellers as the price moves higher. What happened instead, is that the sellers re-grouped and a new battle got underway. In effect, this prolonged impasse between the two sides cancels out the first battle, so whichever way the latest skirmish is resolved determines the course of the next important move. In this case, it is down.

Chart 5.14 represents a one-minute bar of December 1997 corn. It really is too illiquid to be of much use as a chart on which to base decisions. If the bars are increased to 10 minutes, as in Chart 5.15, it is possible to obtain a clearer picture of what is going on. A trading range followed the thick vertical bar on the left of the chart.

This pattern is called a **flag** because it gives the impression of a flag; the sharp (thick) up day being the flagpole and the rectangular trading range being the flag. This type of action is often seen in very strong and sharp rallies or reactions. The flag formation represents a couple of hours of profit taking as emotions die down and the gains are digested. A similar formation develops at the extreme right-hand part of the chart, but this time the flag is formed a little above the flagpole. Flags represent continuation patterns in sharp up- and downtrends. When the price breaks above the flag's resistance trendline, a sharp rally typically follows. These are often good low risk places to enter the market since the ensuing move is usually very profitable. On the other hand, if it proves to be a whipsaw, the stop placed under the lower trendline is not that far away, so any loss will be very small relative to the potential gain.

Finally, take a look at the series of volatile days contained in the ellipse in Chart 5.16. They represent a period of temporary **exhaustion** as market participants become totally worn out from the strong emotions exhibited by such unusually large 10-minute

Chart 5.14 December 1997 Corn 1-minute Bar

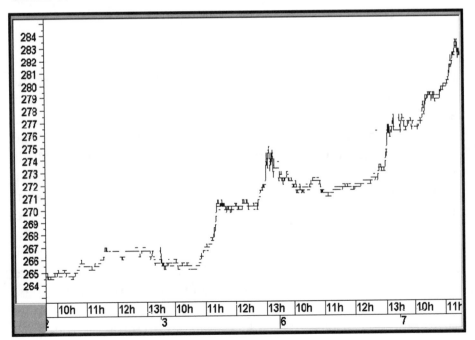

Chart 5.15 December 1997 Corn 10-minute Bar

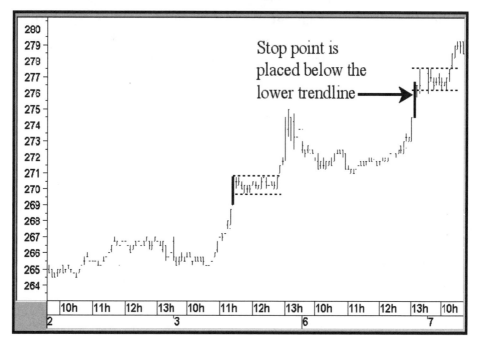

Chart 5.16 December 1997 Corn 10-minute Bar

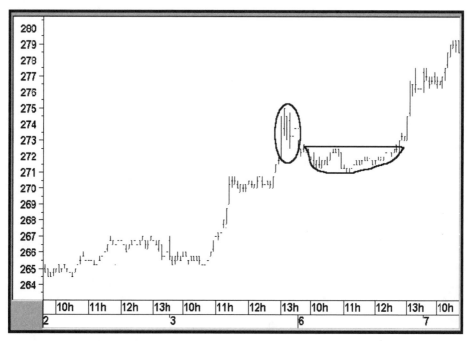

trading ranges. Such action is typically followed by a small sell off and a relatively lengthy consolidation. The pattern, outlined in the chart, is called a **saucer**. Such patterns are well worth watching out for because they represent a very controlled level of profit taking, following which prices typically explode. ■

Chapter 6

One and Two Bar Patterns

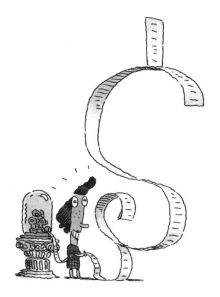

Introduction

One and two bar patterns are much smaller than other patterns described earlier and are, in a sense, characteristics rather than full-fledged price patterns. A prerequisite for all one and two bar formations is that they are preceded by a short-term up or downtrend. This is because these patterns are *short-term* **reversal** phenomena and must have something to reverse. By the time we get to the end of this chapter, you will appreciate that all of these patterns or formations represent *indications of* **exhaustion**, where buyers or sellers have temporarily pushed prices too far up or down and need a rest. During downtrends, *exhaustion* indicates that sellers have exhausted their supply of a particular security and that a temporary halt to the downtrend is likely. When I refer to a temporary halt, or a reversal, the kind of price move I have in mind is about 5 to 20 bars.

Originally, technicians had noted their existence on daily bar charts so these patterns are known as **two-day reversals**. In this tutorial, though, we are concerned with intraday charts so the word **"bar"** seems more appropriate than the word **"day."** With intraday charts it is possible to plot bars at virtually any time frame below that of a day. However, in this section of the tutorial I am featuring 5-minute bars for the most part. Anything less than five minutes does not appear to offer much in terms of the kind of characteristics I will be discussing.

Outside Bars

Outside bars are present when the trading range totally encompasses the trading range of the previous bar. They develop after both down- and uptrends and represent a strong signal of exhaustion. In Chart 6.1, you can see the low was achieved around 13:00 (1 p.m.) and the price zigzagged up for just over an hour. The outside bar is in the vertical rectangle (A), totally encompassing the trading range of the previous bar. Note the opening price developed at a higher level than the previous bar's close, that the closing price of the outside bar was not only down on the period, but even closed below the lowest point of the previous bar. When

Chart 6.1   S&P Composite 5-minute Bar

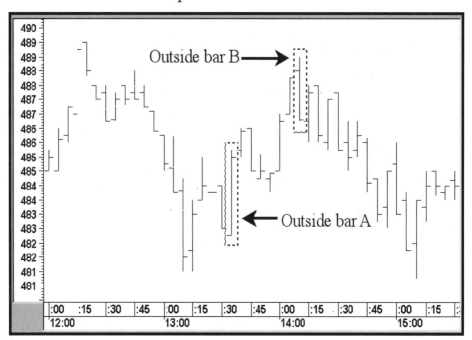

we look at any technical chart pattern it should be interpreted as shades of gray, rather than as black or white. Some patterns offer stronger signs of exhaustion than others do—in other words, not all outside bars are created equal. What we are doing is hunting for clues as to the **degree** of exhaustion being signaled by the reversal bar. I could say the word "help" for example, but if I shout it out from the rooftop, you will get the message that I need help far more clearly. The same principle operates in the marketplace. For example, if the price closes up on the period, it is not as strong a signal as if it closed down. It is saying, "sell," not shouting it. Also, if the outside bar encompasses the trading range of three or four bars it is likely, other things being equal, to be more significant than if it barely encompasses one, and so forth.

If you look carefully, you will see another outside bar being formed at about 40 minutes past the hour at point (B). This time it is a reversal from a downtrend to an uptrend. On the one hand, it does not have much going for it because the outside bar develops after a relatively small decline of about 10 minutes, so there was not much to reverse. However, the price opened on the low and closed pretty close to the high. This means that during this 5-minute period, an important change in psychology had taken place favoring the bulls.

Not all outside bars work, of course, and an **outside bar failure** is shown in Chart 6.2 at (X). It could be argued that the next day started higher and the trend did reverse itself. But who are we fooling? This did not turn out to be a tradable advance at all. It is true the bar was preceded by a pretty good decline, so a stronger up trend could have been expected. However, the opening price was higher and even though the price then went lower, it is not the same "quality" of exhaustion that develops when prices open lower, then go lower, finally closing up on the bar.

Finally, there is one more outside bar on this chart that we need to examine—the one formed during the 14-15:00 (2-3 p.m.) decline at (Y). In this instance, it is a **consolidation** or **continuation** bar. The psychology is very different for these patterns. We come into the bar in a declining phase, but the bar opens on a positive note—on the high, in fact. Then, for the rest of the period, prices decline and the close develops right at the bottom. This is defi-

Chart 6.2   S&P Composite 5-minute Bar

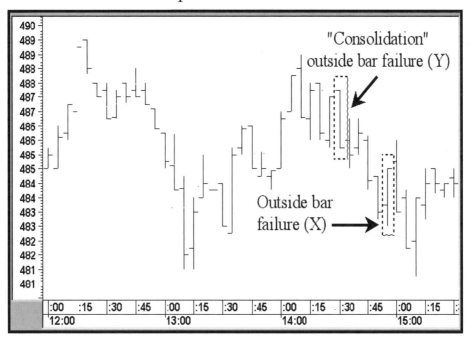

nitely an outside bar, but the fact that it closes so weakly indicated that it is not an exhaustion move in the classic sense.

Chart 6.3 shows the exact same period, but there is no sign of our first outside bar, which developed in the rectangle. This is because I have altered the time frame to a 30-minute bar. I did this to demonstrate that patterns and characteristics, which are present in one intraday time frame, are not necessarily apparent in others. Generally speaking, if a given pattern develops in a 30-minute chart I would give it far greater significance than one that formed in a 5-minute chart.

Inside Bars

Inside bars are the opposite of outside bars, in that the inside bar forms totally within the boundaries of its predecessor. Chart 6.4 is showing a 5-minute bar for the S&P Composite. You can see an inside bar develop in the top left-hand corner. It is not a classic

Chart 6.3   S&P Composite 30-minute Bar

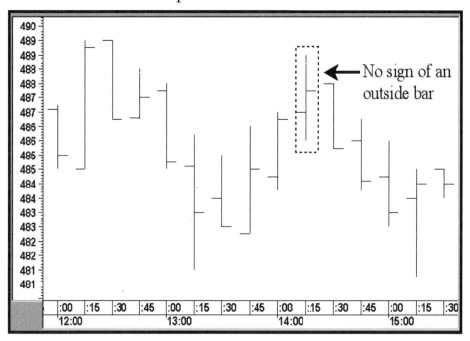

inside bar because the high of the bar, which was set at the opening, is exactly the same as the previous bar. Nonetheless, it does illustrate the point that an inside bar develops after a strong trend and the bar preceding typically has a wide trading range. During this period, buyers or sellers have everything going their way. In this case, it is the buyers because the trend is up. The inside bar is significant because it tells us that the balance between buyers and sellers is now more evenly balanced and that this is the time for anticipating a short-term reversal in trend.

Chart 6.5 shows a more classic example of an inside bar at (A), since it is totally encased within a very long bar. As you can see, it was followed by a very strong and persistent rally. During the advance, we see another inside bar at 14:15 (2:15 p.m.)(B). This is a useful example because (B) was preceded by a worthwhile rally. Why did the price not reverse in this case? Well, remember, the inside bar is really a two bar pattern in which the balance between buyers and sellers experiences a radical change as indicated by the relatively large trading range of the bar, or bars, preceding the inside bar. The preceding bar (A), in this case, is not as large as

Chart 6.4   S&P Composite 5-minute Bar

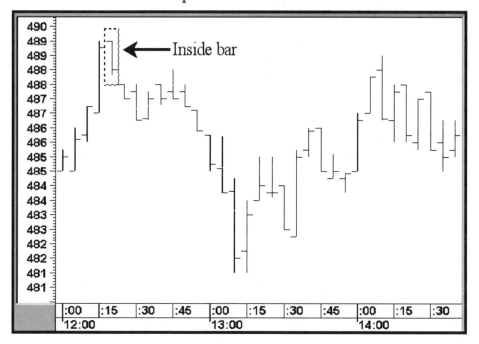

Chart 6.5   S&P Composite 5-minute Bar

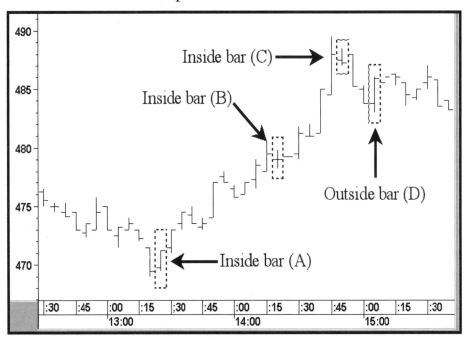

the bar featured in our previous example, so there was no corresponding significant shift from buyers for a more evenly balanced outcome. In short, we are looking for two things in an inside bar. First, it should be preceded by a worthwhile trend, and second, the trading range of the bar preceding the inside bar should be unusually large. That is exactly what happened later at the rally peak as an inside bar (C) develops on the bar after the actual high. Finally, before we leave this chart, you can see an example of a change in trend signaled by an outside bar just after 15:00 (3 p.m.) (D). In this case, the change was from down to sideways.

Two Bar Reversal

A **two bar reversal** is another pattern that signals exhaustion. These patterns develop after a prolonged advance or decline (Chart 6.6). The first bar of the formation (A) develops strongly in the direction of the then prevailing trend. In this example, it is a powerful up bar. For a strong shade of gray we need to see the close of the bar at, or very close to, its high. At the opening of the next period (B), buyers come in expecting more of the same. This means that the price should open very close to the high of the previous bar (C). However, the whole point of the two bar reversal is that a change in psychology takes place as the bar closes slightly above or slightly below the low of the previous bar. Hence, the high expectations of participants at the opening of the bar are totally dashed at the end of the period, indicating a change in trend. To be really effective, this has to be a climactic experience. The two bar pattern really needs to be preceded by a persistent trend and the two bars in question should stand out as having exceptionally wide trading ranges.

Chart 6.7 contains two examples. First, there is a two bar reversal following a rally at (X). The second (Y) appears after a decline. The second bar is quite interesting since it is also an outside bar. The question is whether this qualifies as a two bar reversal or an outside bar? The answer is that it does not really matter because whatever terminology we give this formation, the fact is

Chart 6.6 S&P Composite 5-minute Bar

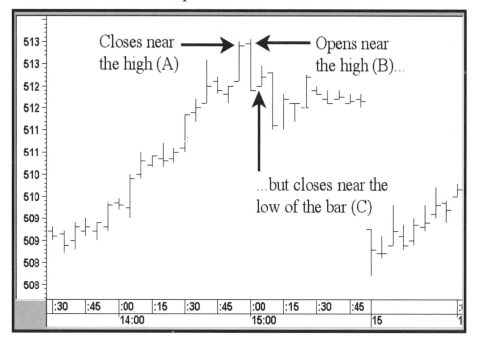

that it indicated an important change in short-term psychology. In effect, this pattern contains the elements of two technical phenomena. Bearing in mind the point I made earlier about shades of gray, this pattern qualifies in spades as a very strong reversal signal. For example, it was preceded by a formidable decline, so there was a lot to reverse. Second, we have the classic characteristics of a two bar reversal. Third, the second bar was an outside bar in its own right.

Key Reversal Bar

A **key reversal bar** is one that develops after a prolonged rally, or reaction. Often this trend will be accelerating by the time the price experiences the key reversal bar.

Chart 6.7   December 1998 S&P Composite 5-minute Bar

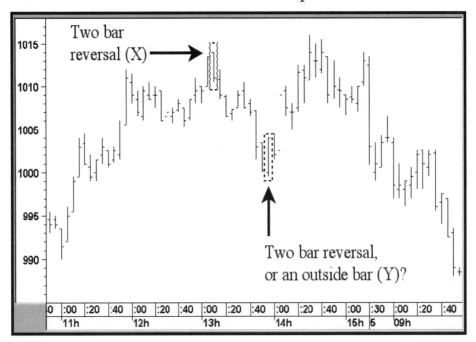

This classic pattern has the following characteristics:

1. The price opens strongly in the direction of the prevailing trend.

2. The trading range is very wide.

3. The price closes close to, or below, the previous close.

4. Volume, if available, should be climactic on the key reversal bar.

The example in Chart 6.8 of the S&P Composite 5-minute bar almost meets all of the qualifications except that the opening is only slightly above the previous close. Even so, this bar does indicate exhaustion. One tip-off is the fact that the upper end of the bar sticks out like a sore thumb above the previous two sessions. In other words, the price broke out strongly to the upside, but was unable to hold its gains, and by the close, had given up ground over the previous period.

Chart 6.8 S&P Composite 5-minute Bar

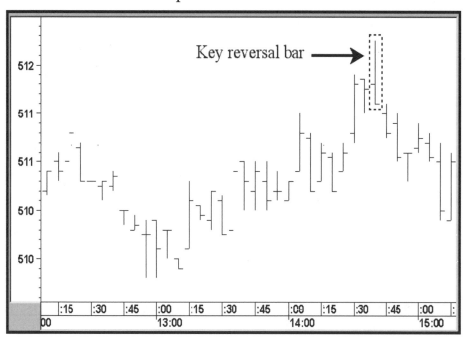

Chart 6.9 features an example of a key reversal bar at a bottom. As you can see, a sharp rally followed this bar, which has two of the characteristics. The price opens way down in the direction of the then prevailing trend (A). It then closes right at the previous close. However, as we move on, you can see that the rally falters and a test of the low takes place (B). Normally, we prefer to see a V-type formation, with the key reversal bar forming the pivotal point. Occasionally there is a quick test, but not usually as pronounced as this. This type of action should raise a red flag concerning the change in psychology supposedly signaled by the key reversal bar. If you look at the bar a bit more closely, you can see that it was not a particularly large one. The trading range should really be much greater, versus the previous bars, in a relative sense, and this one was not. Note how the test of the low was signaled by a mild form of a two bar reversal. I call this "mild" because it is not preceded by a sharp emotional rally. The subsequent reversal was also signaled by a mild two-day reversal. Finally, the price was unable to close above the top of this potential double bottom formation—again, a sign that the key re-

Chart 6.9   December 1998 S&P Composite 5-minute Bar

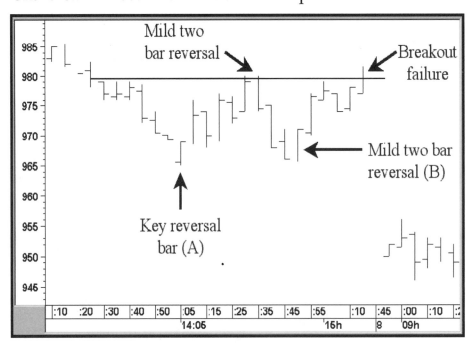

versal bar was not offering all that should have been promised. Also, notice the opening of the next session was sharply lower. We could not have known this was going to take place from the technical position, but the double bottom breakout failure combined with the fact that the test of the key reversal bar almost made a new low were definite ominous signs.

Exhaustion

We have covered quite a bit of material concerning the concept of exhaustion as it appears on the intraday charts. This section will take the discussion a bit further by looking at a few more examples. Look at the huge gap on the opening of the 15th, as depicted in Chart 6.10. You will find that **gaps** almost always develop on the intraday charts at the open due to some overnight change in psychology. In this case, the first bar opens at its high, goes lower, but closes more than halfway up the trading range. This type of activity often indicates exhaustion of selling and can be a precursor to higher prices, at least over the short-term. The key, in such instances, is to see the gap-opening bar sell off quite a bit, and close closer to the high than the low.

Three things to look out for are:

1. A very wide trading range, following a sharp price move

2. The fact that the close is higher than the opening in an uptrend and lower in a downtrend, and

3. That the close is more than halfway up the bar in a downtrend reversal, and more than halfway down in an uptrend reversal.

This example is not that great because the trading range, while reasonable, is not that large. Also, the close is lower than the opening and is barely half way above the mid-point of the bar. Nevertheless, it was able to halt the downward decline in prices.

The example in Chart 6.11 of the NYSE Composite and a 5-minute bar is better, since the trading range is very wide and the close is above the opening. As a result, the price rose for the rest of the morning. If you see a bar like this, are going short, and

Chart 6.10 December 1997 NYSE Composite 5-minute Bar

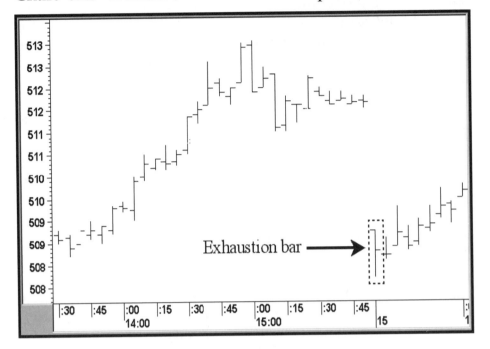

Exhaustion bar ⟶

you have a very short-term time horizon, it certainly makes sense
to cover the position since this is an obvious sign of a reversal in
psychology. Two things to note: First, an inside bar develops after the exhaustion bar, and second, that the rally high, as shown
in this chart, almost closed the gap.

    Chart 6.12 offers another example of an exhaustion bar. It has
two of our elements, an extremely wide trading range and price
closing close to the high. The closing, however, is once again below the opening. This goes back to our shades of gray, for while
the opening/closing characteristic is absent, the wide nature of
the bar, and the fact that the close was close to the high in a pro-
portionate sense strongly indicates this bar reflected a really
significant shift in psychology. You can see it was followed by what
I have termed as an "almost inside bar." "Almost" refers to the
fact that the high is almost identical with that of the exhaustion
bar.

Chart 6.11   December 1997 NYSE Composite 5-minute Bar

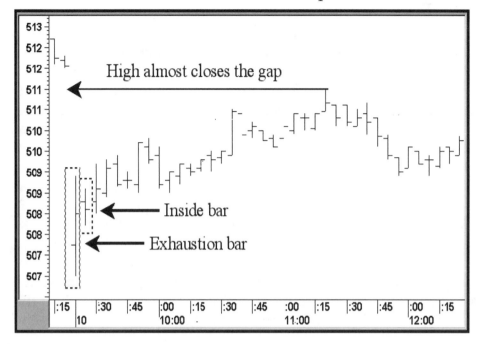

Chart 6.12   December 1997 NYSE Composite 5-minute Bar

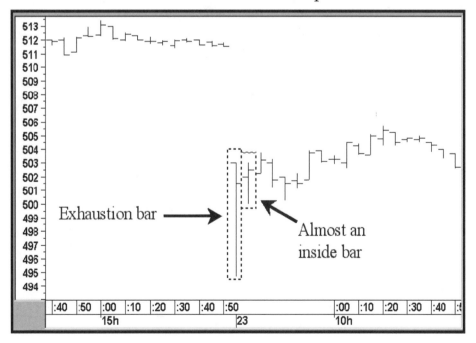

Pinocchio Bars

Exhaustion also shows itself in other forms that are different from the characteristics we have previously explored. I call these **Pinocchio bars**, because they temporarily give us a false sense of what is really going on. They are bars where the bulk of the trading takes place outside the previous and subsequent trading range, and, thus, give a false impression of a breakout. The character Pinocchio tells us when he is lying because his nose gets bigger. With a Pinocchio bar, it is the isolated part of the bar, above the open and close, that is the "big nose." It is this end of the bar that signals a probable false move. An example appears in Chart 6.13. In an uptrend, the bar opens a little higher. Then the price works its way significantly higher, only to close near the opening. If it closes down on the bar, so much the better—from the point of view of the strength and reliability of the signal. Sometimes it even closes below the previous low. The worse the close the stronger the signal, other things being equal. In a sense, the

Chart 6.13 S&P Composite March 1997 10-minute Bar

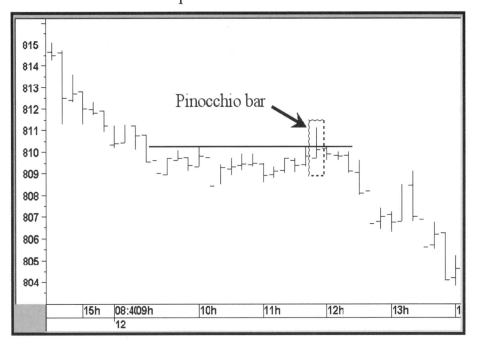

Pinocchio bar is a form of key reversal bar. However, the critical point is that the trading between the opening and closing takes the price much higher than either of the opening and closing prices.

Chart 6.14 shows another example of a Pinocchio bar. In this instance, the price moves below the trading range only to close back within it. Once again, it is possible to construct a line marking the lower part of the range.

In Chart 6.15 a small Pinocchio bar breaks above the previous minor high set 8 bars earlier. However, by the end of the bar, it came right back to the breakout level. At this point, it was not clear whether this was a real Pinocchio bar or not. After all, it would have been cancelled in the event the next bar made a new high. Consequently, the Pinocchio was not confirmed until it was obvious that the next bar or two were unable to rally close to the Pinocchio high. Indeed, you can see that the next two bars actually opened at their high, which happened to be the Pinocchio close. If you are long in a situation like this, the best thing to do is to liquidate when it becomes obvious that a Pinocchio has formed. This may be on the bar itself, or a couple of bars after. It just de-

Chart 6.14   S&P Composite March 1997 10-minute Bar

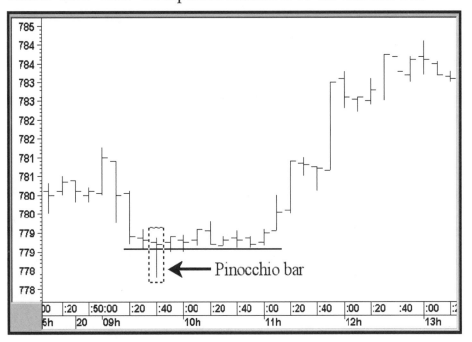

Chart 6.15 NYSE Composite 5-minute Bar

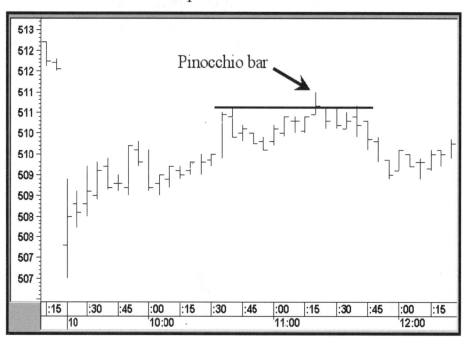

pends on when the Pinocchio becomes obvious; i.e., when it is apparent that the bulk of the trading on the suspected Pinocchio bar is an isolated affair. If it does not turn out to be a Pinocchio, you can easily place a stop to re-enter the position when the price breaks above the suspected Pinocchio high. Generally speaking, the longer the trendline that contains the previous highs in the case of an upside breakout, or lows in the case of a downside one, the stronger the whipsaw.

One important fact about an exhaustion move is that the extremity of the move often proves to be an important support or resistance point. In Chart 6.16, for instance, it was possible to draw a horizontal line at the top of the Pinocchio bar shown in the previous chart, and extend the chart forwards. The support level becomes one of resistance. In fact, the bar that attempted to beat this price almost qualifies as an outside bar, but the low does not quite take out the previous low. In any event, this bar certainly gives the impression of exhaustion since the price opens higher and closes on its low.

Chart 6.16 NYSE Composite 5-minute Bar

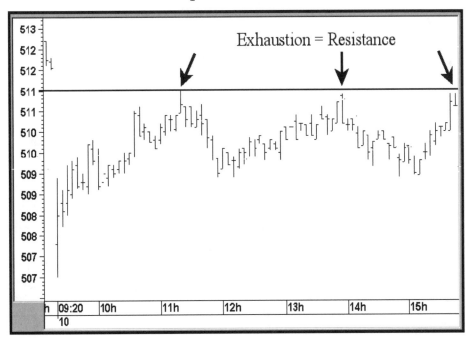

More Examples of One and Two Bar Patterns

Charts 6.17 to 6.19 feature 30-minute bars. The S&P Composite in Chart 6.17 does not have opening prices, so we are left a little in the dark. However, it is worth showing because some of the points we have already discussed are nicely demonstrated. At the close of the 6th, there is an exhaustion bar since the price closes well off a spiky low. After a quick two-hour rally, a test gets underway. You can see that the previous intra-bar exhaustion low, more or less, held the quick test on the bar contained within the rectangle. An outside bar then develops. Even though these are short-term phenomena we would expect to see a longer rally than the one that subsequently developed. Actually, the very next bar gaps up, indicating excitement. This happens to be the first bar of a two bar reversal. This pattern opens up a gap of its own that is quickly closed. Note how

Chart 6.17   S&P Composite 30-minute Bar

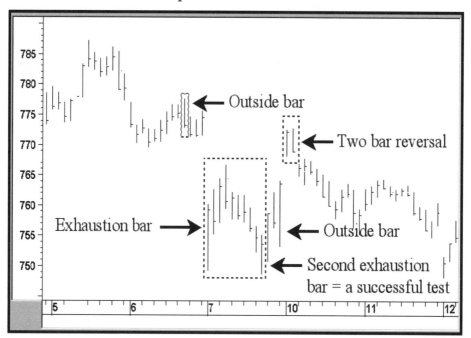

the gap on the 12th is also closed within the first two hours of trading.

One final point worth noting on this chart is the outside bar that developed after a small 5-bar rally in the middle of the 6th in the left-hand part of the chart.

Chart 6.18 shows several outside bars. The first one (A) closes well below the previous bar's low. However, the second one (B) closes in the body of the previous bar, but the stronger encompassing action is certainly indicative of a change in psychology.

Finally, we see two inside bar formations, one on the left-hand part (C) and the other, just a few bars before the chart ends (D). The first one marks a very important intraday bottom. Unfortunately, there are no consistent principles on whether an inside bar will turn out to be a temporary bottom, start of a consolidation, or the beginning of a major rally. They merely serve as an indication that the prevailing trend has come to a temporary halt. A great place perhaps to write options?

Chart 6.19 features a 30-minute bar for December 1997 corn,

Chart 6.18 S&P Composite 30-minute Bar

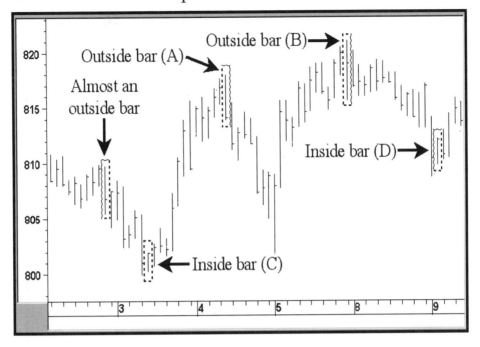

which has some really interesting technical characteristics. Let us begin on the left and work forward. The chart opens with a sharp rally. Then we see what looks to be a two bar reversal. In reality it is not, because the close of the second bar should be close to the opening or low of the first bar. This one was more than halfway up that bar. It did, somewhat, qualify as an inside bar, although an inside bar is normally much smaller relative to the previous bar. In any event, a consolidation did take place and the price broke out from an inverse head and shoulders pattern. However, on the next bar, the price opened close to the previous bar's open, but closed well below its low. This was a great signal, for not only was it a true two bar reversal, but the reversal represented a false breakout from a bullish pattern. Thus, we have two pieces of evidence that the trend had reversed to the downside. The next bar opens with a gap to the downside and the formation of a type of double bottom formation. The bar forming the final low for the move just happens to be an outside bar. Things look good at this point because we have a pattern breakout and an outside bar. All that is required is some more base building and the bearish over-

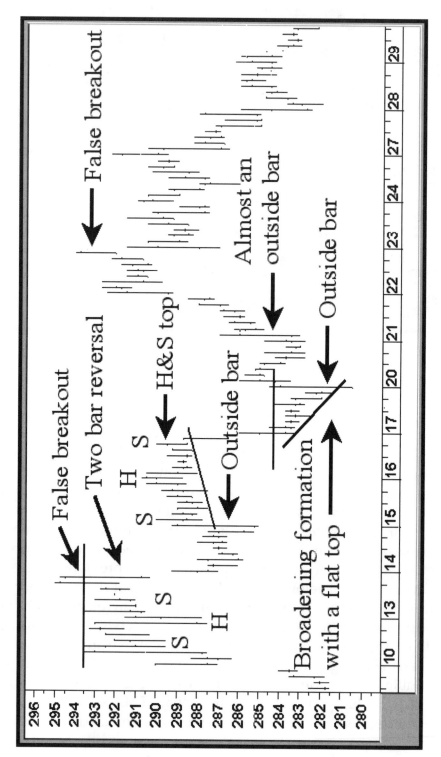

Chart 6.19 December 1997 Corn 30-minute Bar

tones of the failed reverse head and shoulders can be cancelled. That is what appears to be taking place at this point. However, once the gap has been filled, the price starts to slip and actually breaks down from a head and shoulders top. This now cancels the double bottom.

After the price drops, it then consolidates into what turns out to be a broadening formation with a flat top. The declining line roughly corresponds to the broadening part, the horizontal one and this one is the flat top. This pattern is quite rare, but when you spot one, the formation is usually followed by a very strong rally. In this case, the bar of the breakout is also a strong outside bar. I would even go so far as to upgrade it to a key reversal bar since the price opened sharply down on the day and closed in the opposite direction. Note that this bar also encompasses the previous six bars. Obviously, a very significant change in psychology has taken place. After a brief retracement and consolidation, another strong up day confirms that the true trend is up. This is not an outside bar because the low of this bar was above its predecessor. Nevertheless, the open close to the low and the strong rally with the closing near the high was a positive sign.

The next event worth taking note of was this false breakout. This was not a true Pinocchio bar because there was no trading spike above the opening and close. The bar actually closed close to its high. There really was no warning from the chart to get out prior to the next session's sharply lower opening. ∎

Chapter 7

The Significance
of Gaps

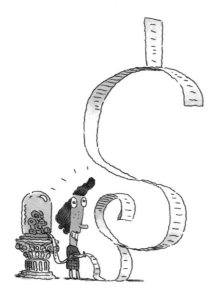

The Concept of Gaps

One of the most intriguing characteristics of technical analysis is the concept of gaps. A **gap** appears on a chart when the trading range of a price bar takes place either totally above or below the trading range of the previous bar. It shows up as a vacuum, or blank space. Gaps do not normally appear on intraday charts that only cover one day's action, unless some dramatic breaking news causes participants to panic either on the up- or downside. Gaps usually develop between the end of one day's trading and the start of the next, as they reflect a sharply higher or lower opening. There is an old Wall Street adage that *the market abhors a vacuum and that sooner, or later, gaps are closed*. This is a correct statement in most instances, but in case you think this is invariably the case, remember that there is a gap in the daily chart of the Dow Jones Industrial Average set in 1932 at around 40—this gap has not yet been closed.

The reason why most gaps are closed is that they are emotional affairs and reflect traders who have strong psychological motivation. We could say excess fear, or greed, depending on the direction of the trend. Decisions to buy or sell *at any cost* are not objective ones, which means the odds of people having second thoughts when things have cooled down, are pretty high. The closing of the gap, or at least a good attempt at closing it in a case of emotion, represents the second thoughts.

The daily bar chart featured in Chart 7.1 shows a true classic gap between the trading ranges of two sessions. As you can see, this gap was quickly closed. However, a gap on two consecutive days on an intraday chart is not a gap in the true sense. For example, in Chart 7.2, the price gapped up at the opening and created a vacuum on the chart. However, if you look at the previous day, you will see that the opening price of the trading range was not exceeded; thus on a daily chart, there was no gap. The two days in question are highlighted with rectangles in Chart 7.3, and there is no gap.

This means that gaps on intraday charts, between opening and closing prices, are far more common than on daily charts. This reduces their significance somewhat, but I still contend that gaps

Chart 7.1   Compaq Computer Daily Bar

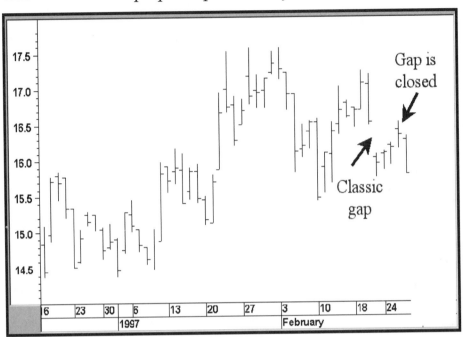

Chart 7.2   March 1997 Bonds 15-minute Bar

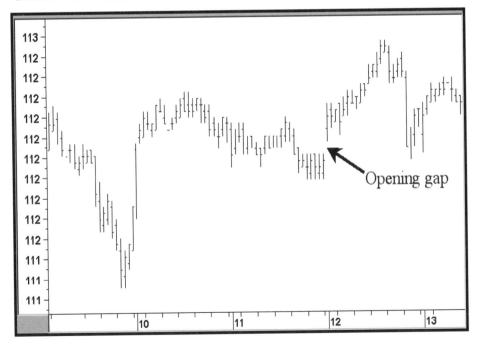

Chart 7.3 March 1997 Bonds 15-minute Bar

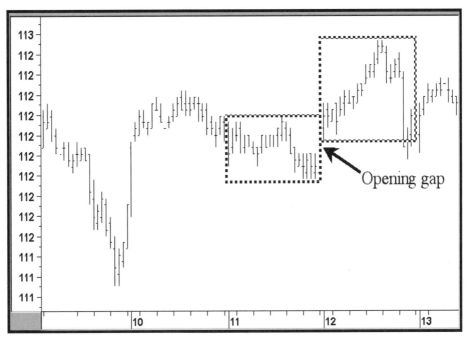

on intraday charts offer important technical characteristics.

Chart 7.4 features a 30-minute bar of the S&P Composite. A gap appears in the chart on the morning of the 7th (A). Prices rise, and as time progresses, you can see that a worthwhile attempt is made to close it at the following day's opening (B). The point is that as long as the gap remains open, the odds favor it being closed within a few sessions. This means that very short-term trades from the long side are less likely to make money than short trades following upside gaps, and vice versa.

Another gap forms on the 11th (C), this time to the downside. This situation looks pretty desperate with the steep decline. What we see, though, is a quick recovery that almost closes the gap (D). In the process, an upside gap is created (E) and later it almost closed (F).

Chart 7.4   S&P Composite 30-minute Bar

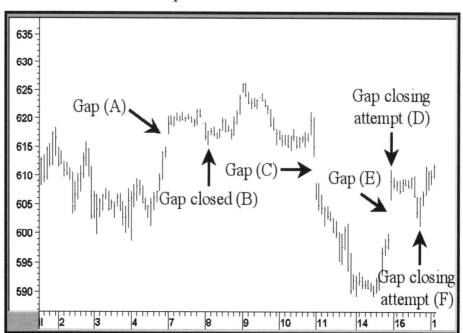

Opening Gaps

There are two types of **opening gaps.** Each can be treated in two different ways depending on your method. A **classic gap** develops as prices open beyond the trading parameters of the previous session (Chart 7.5). The second, more common gap, called an **intrabar gap**, develops in the intraday charts as the opening price of a new day gaps well away from the previous session's closing bar. Intrabar gaps only fall between two bars calculated on an intraday time frame. This gap is far more common because a 15- or 30-minute bar is far smaller than a one-day bar. This means that the empty spaces on the chart are not so great. In effect, these intrabar gaps reflect more subdued emotions. Chart 7.6 shows an intrabar gap (A). Note how all the trading in the rectangle belongs to the previous day's session, so the gap is just a gap in terms of the closing and opening bar. Further to the right is another intrabar gap (B). The low of the opening bar falls at the same level as the high for the previous session and is marked by the rectangle.

Chart 7.5   March 1997 Bonds 15-minute Bar

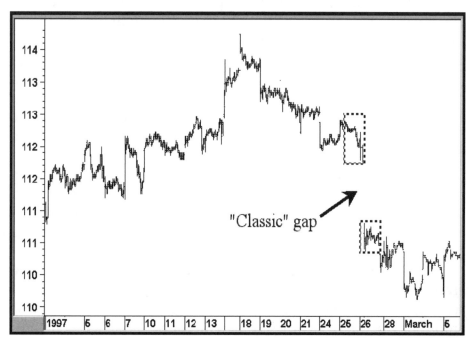

Chart 7.6   March 1997 Bonds 15-minute Bar

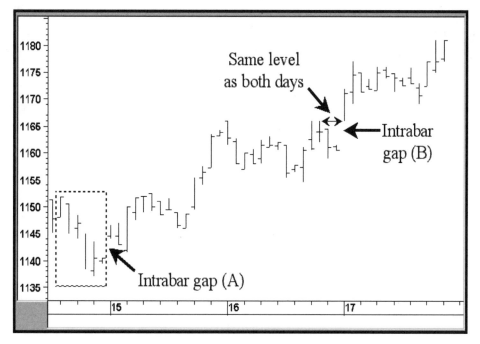

If you are a trader with a two- to three-week time horizon using intraday charts, you should approach gaps differently than if you have a one- or two-day time horizon. If you fit into this latter category, avoid initiating trades at the time the gap is created. This is because almost all gaps are eventually closed. Sometimes this happens within a couple of hours, and with others, it can take two or three weeks. Consequently, if you buy on an opening gap on the upside, as in Chart 7.6, you run the risk that it will soon be closed. The problem is you do not know whether it will be two days or four weeks. The price may well rally sharply, as it did at (A), in Chart 7.7 of March 1999 sugar. Clearly it would have been quite easy to take some profit. Gap (B), on the 11th, was closed on the very next bar. The downside gap at (C) took five days before a reasonable attempt was made at closing it. The gap at (D) was not closed until the sharp rally at the opening of the 29th.

It is important to remember that gaps are caused by strong emotions, where market participants move sharply to the buy or sell side depending on the direction of the trade. Often those emotions run out of steam, so when buyers are exhausted there is

Chart 7.7   March 1999 Sugar

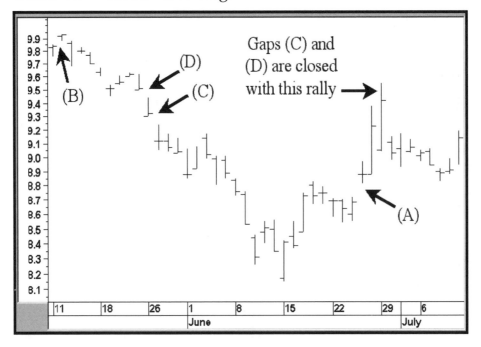

no more buying power left. This means that prices are forced down, either by a lack of buying, or due to pressure from greater selling, as people try to cash in on higher prices.

Intraday Opening Gaps

It makes sense for all traders to step aside when the market opens sharply higher, or lower, unless the gap opening develops close to an important support or resistance area (which can be used to place a close stop). In the case of stocks, **opening gaps** are caused by an order imbalance. In the case of an **upside gap**, the market makers are forced to go short so that they can satisfy the unfilled demand. They naturally try to get the price a little higher at the opening so that it will come down a little, enabling them to cover all, or part, of the short position. The process will be reversed in the case of a lower opening. The key, then, is to watch what happens to the price *after* the opening range. Normally, if prices work their way higher after an upside gap and opening trading range, it will set the tone of the market for at least the next few hours, often longer.

On the other hand, if the price starts to close the gap after a few bars, then the tone becomes negative. For example, Chart 7.8 features a 7.5-minute bar of Merrill Lynch. An opening gap develops at the Wednesday opening (1). After a bit of backing and filling, the price gradually works its way lower throughout the day. The signal that the opening could be an aberration developed after the price slipped below trendline (A), marking the opening range. Note how the trendline proved to be resistance for the rest of the session. Thursday again sees an opening gap (2), but this time there is very little in the way of a trading range since the price continues to climb. Again, the rally away from the opening bar sets the tone for the rest of the day. Later, on Friday, another gap appears (3), but this time the opening trading range is resolved on the downside, as the price breaks below the $86 level flagged by trendline (B). Once again, this proves to be resistance for the rest of the day.

Chart 7.9 features Amazon.com. The gaps are not as dramatic, but the principle still holds. Friday sees a gap to the upside (A), but the price is never able to move above the $124 opening level.

Chart 7.8   Merrill Lynch 7.5-minute Bar

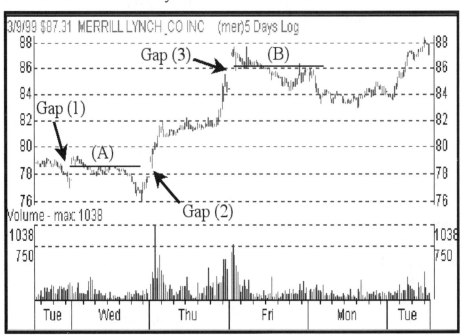

The rest of the day is spent either sideways or in a decline. The opposite is true of the following Tuesday, where an upside gap (B) is followed by a clear-cut trading range. The trading range is then resolved to the upside, as the price breaks above the upper trendline. Note: This gap only appears on the intraday charts since the opening fell within Monday's trading range.

Chart 7.10 features a 15-minute bar for General Motors. A downside gap develops on Monday (1). The price breaks above the high of the opening two bars flagged by trendline (A). This was the signal that prices were unlikely to decline, at least for a few hours. The rest of the day and the following day were then spent recovering the Monday morning losses. On Thursday, the opening gap (2) is quickly followed by a rally above the resistance of the late Friday, Monday, and Tuesday resistance highs, marked by trendline B. While there was no opening range to signal higher prices, the successful penetration of this formidable resistance would have been sufficient evidence to indicate higher prices. Finally, the Friday upside gap (3) offers a bit of an exception to our rule. It is true the price did rally a bit after the opening range

Chart 7.9   Amazon.com 7.5-minute Bar

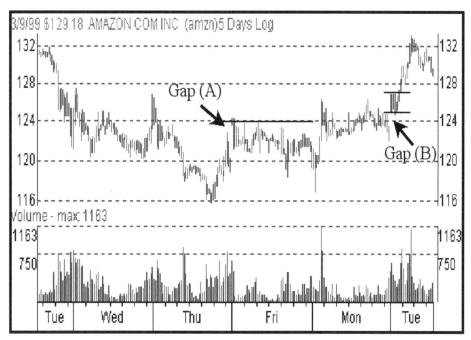

Chart 7.10   General Motors 15-minute Bar

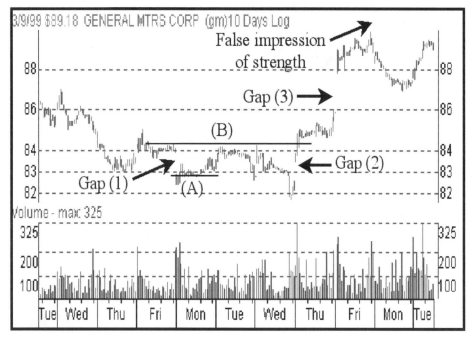

had developed. However, by the close of business, it had fallen back to the lower level of the opening range. I show this last example, purposely, to demonstrate that this opening gap/trading range principle does not work like clockwork. As with all things in technical analysis and human psychology, the odds favor the operation of a principle, but the odds are never 100%. ∎

Moving Averages

The Basics

The use of **moving averages** is a technique that is widely employed by technicians. The objective of moving averages is to smooth out the volatility of raw data. In this way, it is often easier to discover the underlying trend. Buy and sell signals are triggered as the price crosses above and below the trend reflected by the moving average. Moving averages promise a simple solution to a somewhat complex problem—but do they deliver? The answer, I feel, is yes and no. By that, I mean that they are a useful tool, but are certainly not the Holy Grail. I believe moving averages should be used in conjunction with other technical tools. The more indicators that are pointing in the same direction, the greater the probability the signal is valid. Moving averages are just one of those tools. Having said that, let us examine them more closely from the point of view of intraday charts.

Chart 8.1 features a 3-day chart of Microsoft® from the Telescan system. The closings are based on 5-minute bar charts (3-day charts are plotted as 4- to 5-minute charts by Telescan®). The moving average, shown as the smoother line, is constructed from 118 periods—a shade under a nine-hour moving average. In the left hand part of the chart, the crossovers are pretty reliable since the price is trending. However, during Wednesday and Thursday, you can see there is a period when the crossovers are totally useless, due to numerous whipsaws. This is one of the drawbacks of using moving averages on their own. Incidentally, this and most all other moving averages featured in this book are simple moving averages. I use this type because I do not find any special benefits to weighted, exponential, or any other variation of smoothing.

Chart 8.2 shows closing prices based on 30-minute bars for S&P Futures. The average is based on 25 periods or 12 ½ hours. Once again, we find periods where the crossovers worked quite well. On the other hand, the two rectangles contain periods when there were quite a few costly whipsaws. Remember, each time a trade is entered, two costs are involved: **commissions** and **slippage**. They may not amount to very much individually, but when multiplied by countless trades, such expenses can make the difference between a good profit and a small loss.

Chart 8.1   Microsoft 4- to 5-minute Bar

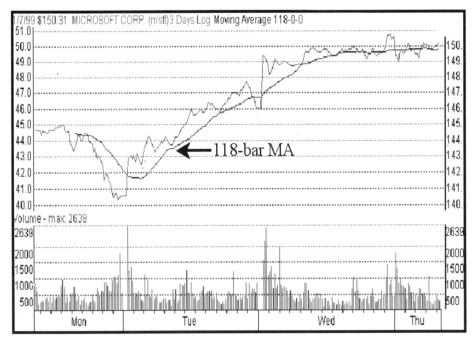

Chart 8.2   S&P Composite 30-minute Bar

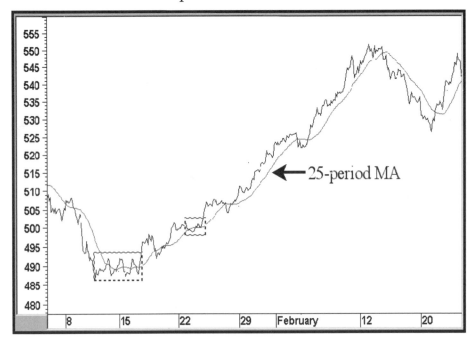

Optimizing

Running the Test

Tick Data® gave me several years of data, so I decided to optimize for the best moving average for the 1996/97 period, using the MetaStock System Tester. For the purposes of the test, I assumed a commission of .02% round trip based on a 50% margin and made no allowances for slippage. Initially, I tested for periods ranging from 6 to 40 bars. Remember, the crossovers are based on the 30-minute bars just using closing prices. The best result came from a 15-period average. Since I had originally tested in steps of three; i.e., every third period, I then ran another test narrowing the information either side of 15, in case there was a better result. In fact, there was, and that was a 13-period, or 6 ½ hours. This was pretty good because 6 ½ hours represent a complete trading day. The results are summarized in Table 8.1. As you can see, there were a total of 946 trades from both the long and short side, about half of which were profitable. That is not a bad ratio. The profit earned was just under 300%. Table 8.2 shows more details.

Table 8.1   S&P Composite 30-minute Close

est...	Status	Net Pr...	Perce...	Tota...	Win...	Losi...	Avg...	OP...
OK	2.7463	274.63	946	302	644	2.6651	13
OK	2.6521	265.21	904	282	622	2.7255	14
OK	2.4135	241.35	856	264	592	2.7801	15
OK	2.0592	205.92	1060	344	716	2.4851	11
OK	1.8917	189.17	1028	323	705	2.6312	12
OK	1.6604	166.04	1154	356	798	2.6334	10
OK	1.6268	162.68	818	242	576	2.8205	16
OK	1.2457	124.57	780	230	550	2.8463	17
OK	0.8755	87.55	761	220	541	2.7985	18

For instance, the average win/lose ratio was 2.67. This means that the average winning trade beat the average losing trade by a factor of 2½. The annual percentage of profit earned was 127%.

   Chart 8.3 shows the equity line based on the 13-period average crossover in the top panel. The system started out with a $1 investment at the close in 1995 and increased to $374 by the end of 1997. It looks pretty good, but remember, there was a 5-month period when profits were flat in 1996 (A); then another 3-month period in the beginning of 1997 (B), followed by an 8-month drought for the rest of the year (C). If you are sitting in front of a screen all day long and not making money for eight months this could get pretty frustrating. Not only that, but also such frustration would most likely result in the abandonment of the system. That is why I believe moving averages are better used in conjunction with the other technical tools described here, such as trendlines, peak and trough analysis, support and resistance, and price patterns.

Table 8.2 S&P Composite 30-minute Close

Total net profit	2.75 Open position value	-0.01
Percent gain/loss	274.63 Annual percent gain/loss	127.69
Initial investment	1.00 Interest earned	0.00
Current position	Short Date position entered	12/31/97
		14:30:000
Buy/Hold profit	1.32 Days in test	785
Buy/Hold pct gain/loss	131.68 Annual B/H pct gain/loss	61.23
Total closed trades	946 Commissions paid	0.45
Avg profit per trade	0.00 Avg Win/Avg Loss ratio	2.67
Total long trades	473 Total short trades	473
Winning long trades	163 Winning short trades	139
Total winning trades	302 Total losing trades	644
Amount of winning trades	13.80 Amount of losing trades	-11.05
Average win	0.05 Average loss	0.02

Chart 8.3 S&P Composite vs. Optimized Equity Line

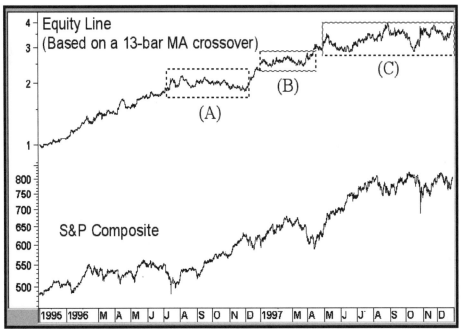

Moving Averages and Price Bars

You may have been wondering why I have been using moving average crossovers in conjunction with closing prices rather than price bars. The reason is that the bars tend to offer a substantial number of whipsaws even though the crossovers are timelier. It is really a question of taste, and with what you feel comfortable. For example, Chart 8.4 features 30-minute bars. It has an excellent crossover signal (A) if we just use the right tick indicating the closing price. It also experiences a couple of whipsaws as well on the 12th (B). However, if I base the signal on bar crossovers, as opposed to the closing price, I am faced with numerous whipsaws, as indicated in Chart 8.5. The closing prices are not always that great, but bar crossovers are even worse. How do we get around these problems? Well, there is no easy answer. The best approach is what I call **guerilla warfare**.

Chart 8.4   S&P Composite 30-minute Bar

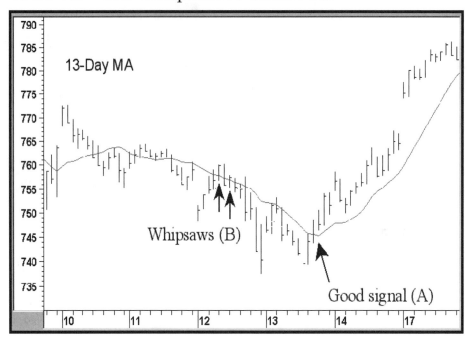

Guerilla Warfare

By this, I mean, rather than allowing moving average crossovers, or any other technical tool for that matter, choose when you should buy and sell, you make the judgment yourself using several indicators simultaneously.   In technical analysis we are always dealing with probabilities, so the more indicators pointing in the same direction, the greater the probability the signal will be valid.   For example, in the rectangle containing some of the whipsaw signals in Chart 8.5, we have just one piece of evidence that the trend has reversed and that is the moving average crossover. What differentiates every one of these crossovers from the profitable signal on the late afternoon of the 13th? The answer lies in the fact that it was also associated with a small trendline break, shown in Chart 8.6, which offers a second piece of evidence that the trend had reversed.   We can actually take this a step further.   Chart 8.7 shows the same period, but this time I have introduced a 13-period **Chande Momentum Oscillator (CMO)**.

Chart 8.5   S&P Composite 30-minute Bar

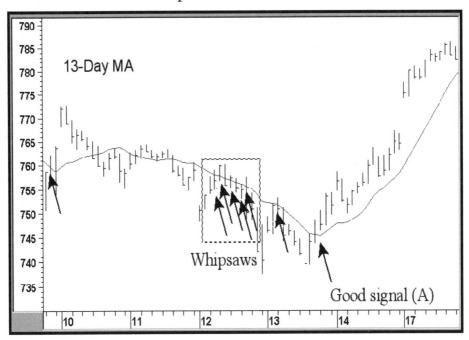

Chart 8.6   S&P Composite 30-minute Bar

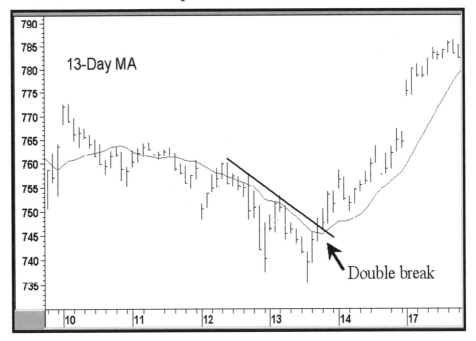

Chart 8.7   S&P Composite 30-minute Bar

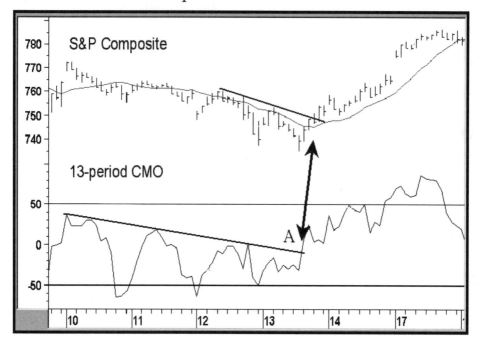

This indicator had previously broken above a fairly long down trendline at (A). Since the MA crossover and the trend break in the price later confirmed this break, it provided the third leg in the bullish stool. The Chande Momentum Oscillator, for those of you who may not have run across it before, is a variation on the RSI indicator.

Working along the same lines, Chart 8.8 features the RSI. I am using it in the same way as the CMO in the previous chart. Between the 30th and 31st there were numerous whipsaw moving average crossovers. Then, the sell signal, late in the middle of the 31st, was confirmed by a trend break in the RSI, plus a trendline violation by the price (A). Later on, the price rises again, and we see more examples of whipsaws. Then, there are two trendline violations at the time of the moving average crossover on the 7th (B). I will have more to say on the idea of using momentum indicators and trendlines in the next couple of chapters. ■

Chart 8.8   S&P Composite 30-minute Bar

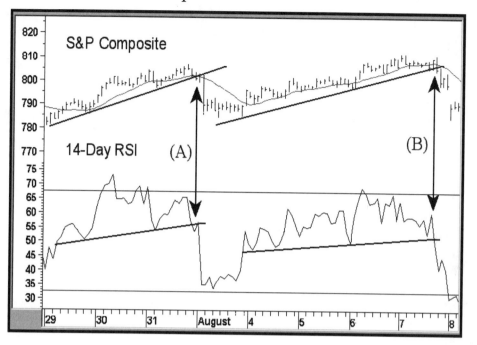

Chapter 9

Applying Oscillators
to Intraday Charts

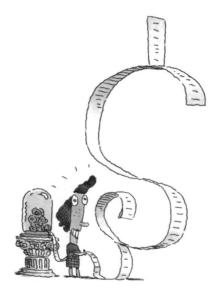

Basic Principles

Oscillators are an extremely useful tool for letting us know when a market or stock is overextended, either on the upside or the downside. In technical analysis, oscillators fall under the generic term **momentum**. Oscillators include many different indicators, most of which are really statistical variations of the price. Occasionally, volume is also incorporated in their formulae. There are several principles for interpreting momentum. Each one applies to all oscillators in some form or another, but the design of specific oscillators means that individual interpretive principles will apply more to one indicator than another.

Overbought/Oversold

Momentum measures the velocity of a price move, either on the upside or the downside. These indicators are usually plotted below the price series being monitored, as in Figure 9.1. They continually move from one extreme to another, rather like an unruly dog on a leash running from one side of the sidewalk to another. When overextended on the upside, the indicator is said to be **overbought**, and on the downside **oversold**. The line in the middle, at zero, is the **Equilibrium Line**. It marks the demarcation between upside and downside momentum. When a momentum indicator reaches an oversold condition, it does not necessarily mean that the price trend is about to reverse. However, it does tell us that it is a good place for taking partial profits from a short position. This is because an indicator that moves to an oversold condition often moves beyond that point. Consequently, it makes sense to wait for the oscillator to rally back above the oversold zone. When that happens, it usually indicates that the *trend of momentum* has reversed, and that is the time to look for a **confirmation from the price**. This could take the form of a moving average crossover, trendline violation, or price pattern completion, etc. Unfortunately, when momentum is oversold, the news is usually bad and the last thing we want to be thinking about is buying. To be successful in all trading and investing, we must look beyond the crowd and the current headlines and buy when things look the blackest.

Figure 9.1 Momentum vs. Price

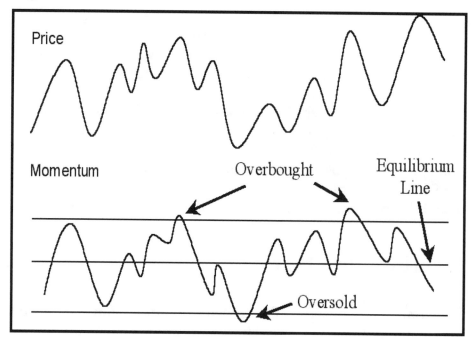

When a momentum indicator reaches an overbought level, it does not guarantee a reversal to the downside, but indicates that the risk/reward does not favor new purchases. It is, though, a place to be thinking about taking profits, or actually taking partial profits. Unfortunately, when momentum is overbought, the news background is favorable and it is a natural human tendency to hang on. Once again, though, success usually comes by going against the crowd, never with it.

Negative and Positive Divergences

Momentum often leads price. Figure 9.2 shows that the price and momentum are rising in concert up to point (C). At points (D) and (E) the price continues its series of higher peaks, but the oscillator does not. This tells us that while the trend looks good on the surface, underneath upside momentum is dissipating and this is not a healthy sign. These non-confirmations by the oscillator are known as **negative divergences**. While they warn that the technical position is deteriorating, they do not, in and of themselves, represent actual sell signals. After all, at this point you do not know how many more divergences are yet to come. Point (D) or (E) could have been the final peak, or there could be a few more rallies before the final high. The trick, once again, is to wait for these divergences to be confirmed by some kind of price reversal trend signal in the price. This is shown in Figure 9.3, as the price breaks below a trendline constructed from the lows in the price.

The opposite is true at market bottoms where a situation in which the price makes a series of lower lows and the momentum does not is known as a **positive divergence**. An example is featured in Figure 9.4. In this instance, as the price is declining, the oscillator is literally walking uphill. Once again, this is a positive signal and must be confirmed by a trend reversal signal in the price.

Figure 9.2 Negative Divergence

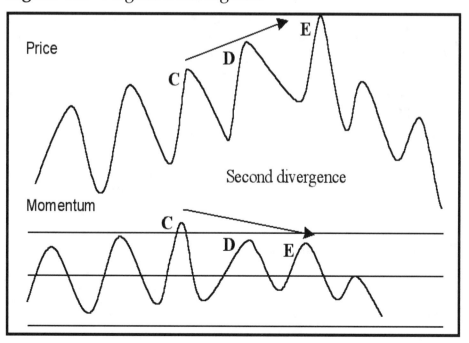

Figure 9.3   Confirmation by the Price

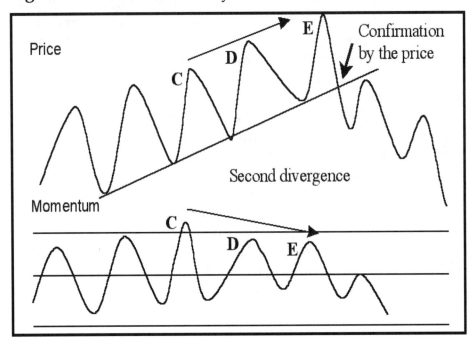

This is how it might work. Figure 9.5 features a positive divergence (1). We may be tempted to buy at A, because we can see a positive divergence. However, the price is below the moving average and has not confirmed this positive momentum configuration. As you can see, it would have paid to wait, since the price declined and another positive divergence appeared (2). As it turned out, the moving average crossover developed at a lower price. Had there been another divergence, the moving average would have saved us even more money. Figure 9.5 also shows that it was possible to construct a trendline (3).

Consequently, there were three pieces of evidence that the trend had reversed: 1) the positive divergences, 2) confirmation by the moving average crossover, and finally, 3) the trendline break.

To summarize the main points:

1. Momentum is a generic term that includes all oscillators

2. The principles of momentum interpretation apply to all momentum indicators in one form or another

Figure 9.4 Positive Divergence

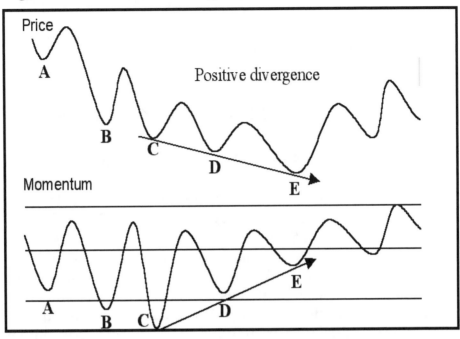

Figure 9.5 Trendline Construction with a Divergence

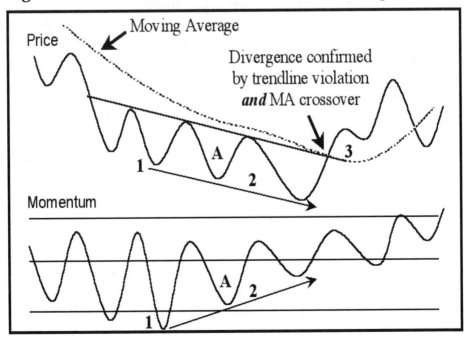

3. Two momentum principles are overbought/oversold cross-overs and positive and negative divergences, and

4. Momentum signals should always be confirmed by a trend reversal signal in the price.

Time Frames and Momentum Signals

A **rate of change indicator** (ROC) is calculated by dividing the price "n" periods ago by the latest plot. Table 9.1 shows an example for the calculation of a 12-month ROC. The first step is to divide the price of 105 for January by the price 12 months ago, which is the January of the previous year; in this instance 99. This gives us a ROC plot of 106. Then, February at 100 is divided by February a year ago of 110, for a reading of 90.9 and so forth. Most of the time, the ROC is plotted as a plus and minus number, so that 106 translates into +6, - 90.6 = - 9.4, and so forth. The equilibrium line would change from 100 to 0. The time span, under consideration, can have a very important effect on the size of any ensuing price move. For example, an overbought reading from an oscillator calculated from a very long-term time span is much more significant than an oscillator calculated from a relatively smaller time span. That is because it is monitoring a longer-term trend, which the shorter-term oscillator may not be able to pick up. In Chart 9.1, featuring the Japanese yen and a 12-month ROC, an overbought condition is likely to signal a maturing bull market where the subsequent bear market may last for a year or more. An oversold condition is also likely to be followed by a long-term move. On the other hand, the overbought condition in the 30-day ROC for J P Morgan in Chart 9.2 is only followed by a two-month decline. Similarly, the oversold reading results in a 3-month rally. You can see, then, that a substantially smaller momentum time frame results in substantially smaller moves.

The same principle is true for intraday charts; the longer the time spans of the oscillators, the greater the significance of any given signal. Chart 9.3 features the S&P Composite with a 30-minute close and a 10-period ROC. The rallies and reactions following overbought/oversold conditions average about 2 ½ days. On the other hand, Chart 9.4, a 5-minute close-only chart

Table 9.1   Calculation for a 12-month ROC

Month	Price	ROC
January	99	
February	110	
March	115	
April	125	
May	116	
June	119	
July	112	
August	115	
September	100	
October	106	
November	100	
December	112	
January	105	106
February	100	90.9

Chart 9.1   Japanese Yen and a 12-month ROC

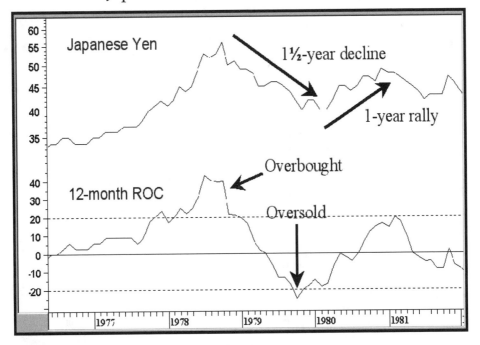

with 10 periods, experiences reaction times following overbought/ oversold conditions of about half a day.

There is another way that differing time spans can be very useful. **Price**, at any one time, is determined by the interaction of a number of different time cycles. A specific momentum indicator, such as a **ROC** or **RSI** (relative strength indicator), can only reflect the limited scope of such cycles. However, if we place two or three momentum indicators on one chart, several different time cycles are reflected. Generally speaking, the greater the numbers of cycles acting in concert, the stronger the price move. In this context, we must assume that the longer the cycle, the greater the implied move. This common action of cycles can be reflected in momentum indicators. For example, Chart 9.5 shows a 9- and 65-period RSI. This is a very popular oscillator, which is a front-weighted, price/velocity ratio for a specific security. It is a momentum indicator that compares the price of a security relative to itself and is relative to its past performance. Its two principal advantages are: 1) it is always contained within the boundaries of 0 to 100, unlike the ROC, which is infinite on the upside, and 2)

Chart 9.2   JP Morgan and a 30-day ROC

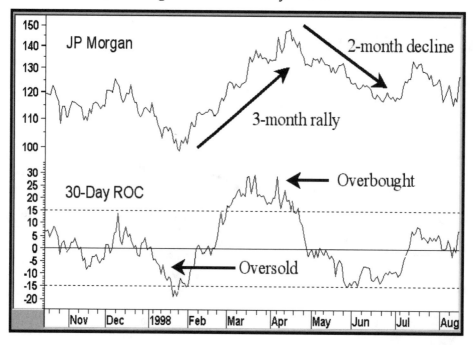

Chart 9.3   S&P Composite 30-minute Close

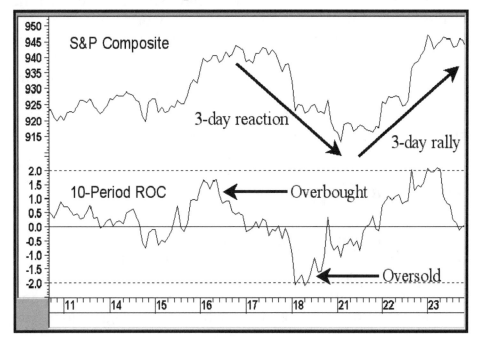

Chart 9.4   S&P Composite 5-minute Close

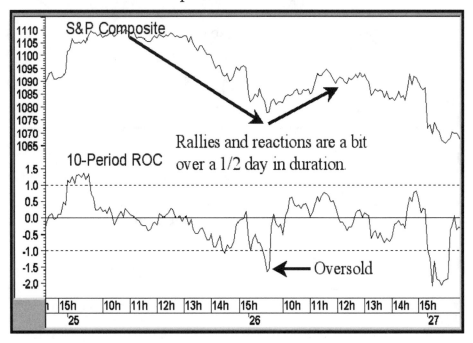

the nature of the calculation allows easy comparison between two different securities. The reason why I have shown these two time frames is that, on occasion, one of them may bring out characteristics that the other does not. For example, the 9-day series is oversold at (A), but the price does not rally. Instead, it moves sideways. This is because the 65-period RSI, which monitors longer-term, and, therefore, more dominant cycles, is barely below the 50-equilibrium level. This fact would not have been apparent had we not been looking at two different time frames.

Trendline Construction

Oscillators, just like price, move in trends. Trend reversal signals in oscillators are given in the same way. In other words, oscillators experience moving average crossovers, and occasionally form price patterns, etc. However, one of the simplest and most effective tools with oscillators that are very jagged in nature

Chart 9.5   S&P Composite 5-minute Close

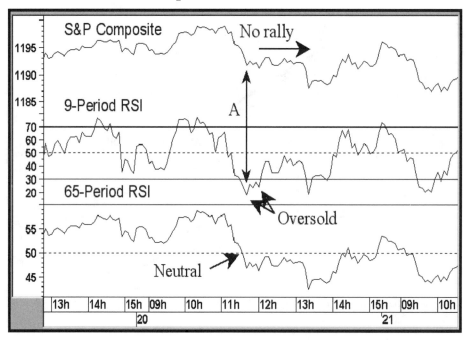

is the use of **trendline violations**. Figure 9.6 shows how it is possible to construct a down trendline. When it is violated, a reversal in the **momentum trend** is signaled. This is not an actual signal to buy or sell, because you cannot buy and sell momentum. However, it does tell us that the prevailing momentum trend has reversed, and that the underlying technical structure is getting stronger. The next thing to look out for is a trend reversal signal in the price, since this will confirm the stronger momentum. This could be a moving average crossover, or even a price pattern completion. However, I find the simplest and most effective signal is a **trendline violation**, as shown in Figure 9.6. Such penetrations occasionally develop simultaneously with a momentum trend break, but more often it will occur with a small lag. Let us look at a couple of examples.

Figure 9.6 Down Trendline Construction

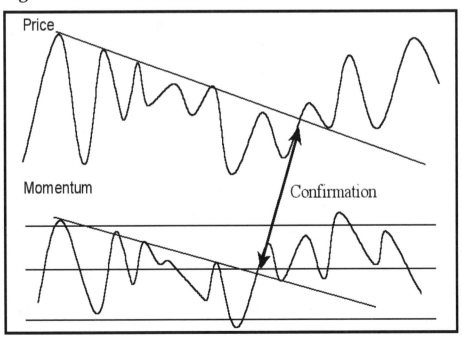

Examples of Momentum/Price Trendline Violations

Chart 9.6 features a 5-minute bar with a 45-period ROC. The bulk of the trading action is devoted to a strong rally. Note that as the price works its way higher, the peaks in the ROC become lower and lower. These are negative divergences. However, this just indicates weakening momentum in the same way as a house beam being eaten by termites. In the beam analogy, you know that the structure is getting weaker and weaker, but you do not know when it is weak enough to fall until it signals this fact by actually crumbling and falling. In this case, the momentum trend reversal signal is a violation of a more or less horizontal line at the zero. As it happens, it is simultaneously confirmed by a trend break in the price. This event is then followed by a nasty decline.

In Chart 9.7, we see a 25-period ROC of the closing price of the S&P Composite 5-minute bar. The uptrend in momentum is broken before the uptrend of the price. You may wonder why I have

Chart 9.6   S&P Composite 5-minute Bar

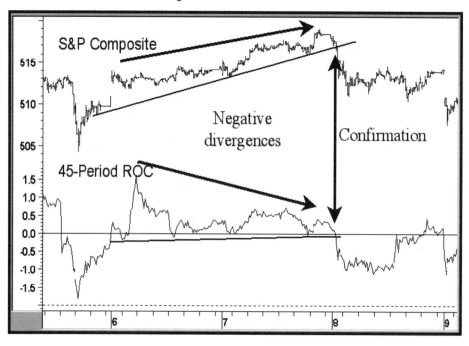

constructed the trendline so that it cuts through the low marked by the arrow (A). Remember, the objective of drawing a trendline is to catch the underlying trend. When you draw a trendline, you can see how many times it has been touched or approached, since this will determine its significance as a support or resistance level. In this case, we have one whipsaw, at A. However, apart from this one discrepancy, the line is very good as a dynamic level of support. Obviously, I would prefer to have a clean line that has not been violated at all, but, in this case, I have to settle with a less than perfect scenario, because that is still the best reflection of a support level.

Now let us look at it another way. If support had been at a specific number, say $100, and the price had fallen to $100 several times, I would still regard $100 as a good support level even if the price did whipsaw down to $99 on one occasion. It makes any breakdown a bit iffy, but I would rather settle for $100 than nothing at all.

Chart 9.7 S&P Composite 5-minute Bar

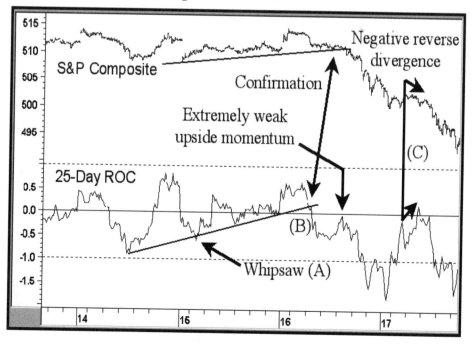

There are several other interesting points to note. First, even though the price remained reasonably close to its high after the momentum trend break (B), the ROC was never able to get back above zero until the 17th when the price was significantly lower. That, in and of itself, indicated weakness. The chart also reveals an example of what I term a **reverse divergence**. Remember, during a rally, momentum is supposed to peak out ahead of the price. On the extreme right hand part of Chart 9.7, it is price that leads momentum. This, too, is an out of gear situation and indicates that the underlying trend is not sound. See how the price makes a second peak lower than the first, but the momentum moves to a new high at the second peak (C). This raised the question that if the price could not rise with expanding momentum, what would make it rise? The answer, in this case, was nothing, since the price continued to retreat. ■

Chapter 10

Integrating Oscillators, Moving Averages and the Parabolic Indicator

Introduction

We never know, in advance, whether forthcoming price action will develop into a trend, or a trading range. Consequently, if we rely on a trend following system, such as a **moving average crossover,** and the price action turns out to be a trading range, we are likely to lose money. This is because the trading range will result in a substantial number of false moving average crossover signals. On the other hand, if the market trends, but we are only using momentum signals, a substantial part of the profit may be given up, since the momentum signal will often take us out too early.

A solution to this dilemma is to split the trade into two parts. The first unit is traded on the assumption of a ranging market, the other on the assumption that the price will experience a good trend. Trading decisions on the first unit would be based on a momentum indicator and those for the second, on a moving average crossover.

One way of executing this trading strategy is to enter the initial position as the price crosses its moving average. Buy on a positive crossing; sell short on a negative crossing. Profits for the first unit are taken when the momentum indicator reaches an overbought zone for long trades, or an oversold level for short trades. The second unit is liquidated as the price crosses its moving average again. If the oscillator fails to move to an overbought or oversold condition, both units are liquidated simultaneously when the price crosses the moving average. The following example will use a price oscillator to demonstrate this strategy.

The Price Oscillator

Chart 10.1 shows a 30-minute S&P bar together with a 30-period price oscillator. The oscillator is constructed by dividing the close of a 30-minute bar by a 30-period moving average of the close. As the price crosses the moving average, the oscillator in the lower panel moves below zero. When the price re-crosses the average, the oscillator moves into positive territory. The zero line represents the moving average. This means that when the price

Chart 10.1   S&P Composite 30-minute Bar

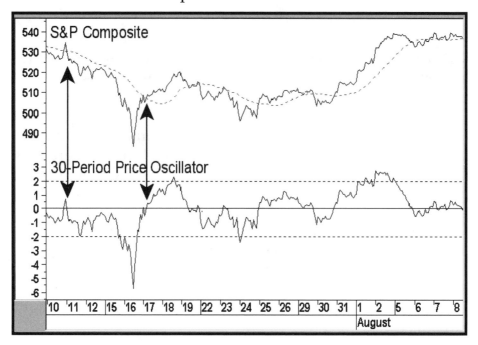

moves a long way above the average, the oscillator registers an overbought condition and vice versa. This is really another way of representing envelopes, or bands, around the price, as shown in Chart 10.2. These envelopes are plotted 2% above and below the 30-period moving average. The overbought and oversold extremes for the oscillator are plotted at plus and minus 2%. Look at point (A), where the oscillator crosses above its overbought zone. The price also moves above its envelope. Then, when the oscillator crosses back below the overbought line on its way back to zero, or the moving average at (B), the price itself also crosses its envelope as it works its way back towards the moving average.

Remember the rule of our two-unit trading strategy. Go long when the price crosses above the 30-period moving average, and then, liquidate the first unit when the oscillator moves to the overbought zone of plus 2%. The second unit is sold as the price crosses below its moving average, which in this case, has a time span of 30 periods. In this particular instance, the oscillator sell signal generates more profit. This is because the price reverses direction so quickly, once it reaches the overbought zone, that a substantial

Chart 10.2   S&P Composite 30-minute Bar

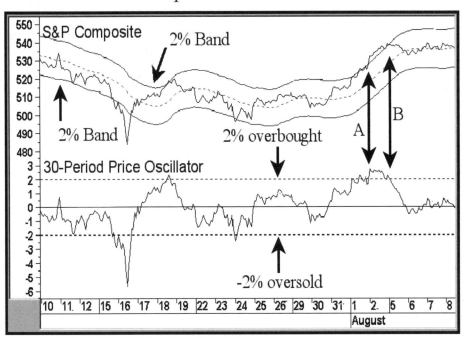

amount of paper profit is given up by the time it recrosses the moving average again. Of course, it is always possible to shorten the time span for the average, but this usually results in too many costly whipsaws.

Now look at what happened after the buy signal at (A) on Chart 10.3. The oscillator moved to an overbought condition well before the final peak in price, so the first unit was sold prematurely at (A₁). Once it had peaked, the price sold off a little, and then crossed below its moving average at (A₂). In this instance, the decline was contained sufficiently to beat the oscillator signal. So, profits were earned in both examples. In one instance, the oscillator was better, and in the other the moving average crossover proved to be superior. That is why a compromise approach, using both techniques, appears to work the best of all under most market environments. Other buy and sell points are also shown on the chart.

You may be wondering why I chose the 2% level for the overboughts and oversolds. This was based merely on trial and error. I know I am never going to get the perfect fit, be it 1%, 2%,

Chart 10.3 S&P Composite 30-minute Bar

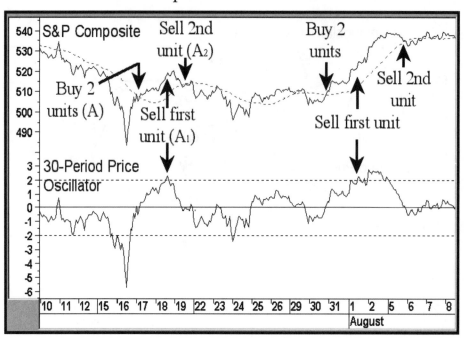

5%, or 6.95683%. What I am looking for is something that is going to work well *most of the time*. The size of the swings in the price oscillator will depend on two things: 1) the volatility of the security, and 2) the selected time span. Since the volatility of each security is different, the level of the overbought/oversold will change, as necessary.

Chart 10.4 reflects a tick plot of December 1998 corn. You can see that it never reaches above 1.5%. It is also evident that the 30-period time span for tick charts is not suitable because of undue volatility.

Chart 10.5 shows that same data, but this time for a 240-period span. You can see that this indicator is far less jagged and undergoes cyclical swings between the overbought and oversold levels. I have drawn the overbought and oversold lines at plus and minus 1% because that seems to be the place that catches most of the rallies and reactions.

As I mentioned before, the longer the time span for any given oscillator, the greater the swing. Overbought and oversold lines should be drawn in such a way that they capture most of the larger

Chart 10.4   December 1998 Corn Tick

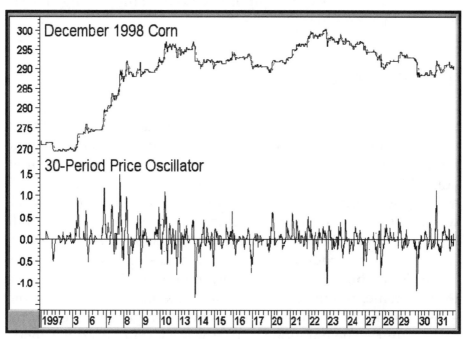

Chart 10.5   December 1998 Corn Tick

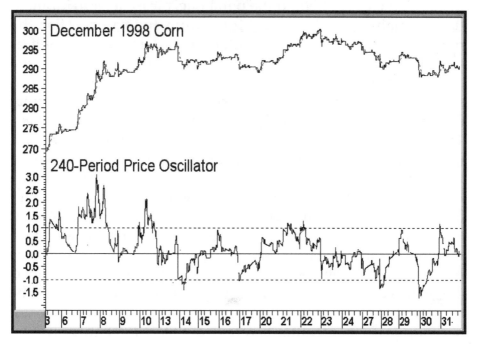

swings, so you can be sure (except for major rallies or reactions) the odds favor an overbought or oversold reading being close to the final turning point.

The Parabolic Indicator

Waiting for moving average crossovers can sometimes be extremely frustrating. Using the moving average crossover to liquidate the second part of the position after an extreme reading, you will recall, often means giving up a lot of the potential profit as the price declines from the ultimate peak of the rally. It is always possible to shorten the time frame of the average, but while the signals would be timelier, many of them would be costly whipsaws. One way around this is to employ a stop, based on Welles Wilder's **Parabolic System**, but only after the oscillator has moved to an extreme, and the first unit is liquidated. In effect, you would substitute the parabolic for the moving average crossover for the second unit. The parabolic indicator is basically used for generating points at which to place stops. An example is shown in Chart 10.6. It is calculated in such a way that the stop is placed more aggressively once a move has built up some momentum. For the theory and concept behind the parabolic, please refer to <u>Momentum Explained—Advanced Momentum Indicators</u>. For the purpose of this book, it is important to understand the application of this useful indicator. The parabolic curve is plotted in the chart as a solid line that is continually crossing the price. You can see how, in most instances, it starts off in an almost horizontal fashion, and then it gradually picks up steam as the price rallies. This is the parabolic characteristic. First we establish a buy point (A). I am using a parabolic penetration, but normally we would use a moving average crossover. The stop is placed just under the indicator, for example, at point (B). For short sales, the stop would be above it (C). This indicator is particularly suitable for placing timely stops once the price starts to accelerate to the upside, since it follows progressively closer to the price. Then, when the price finally crosses below the parabolic curve, the position is stopped out, in this case, pretty close to the top (D). The process would be repeated in reverse for a short position. Since it requires some underlying price momentum before it can start the parabolic pro-

Chart 10.6 S&P Composite 30-minute Close

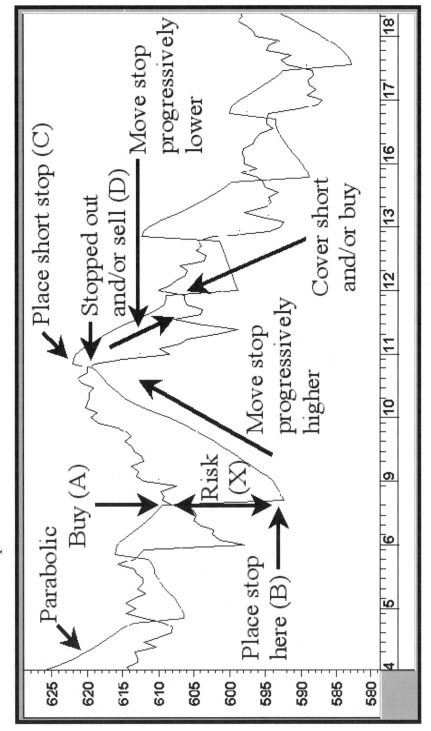

cess, I believe it is better used as a liquidation technique *after* the price oscillator has reached an extreme level. That, of course, is our signal establishing that the trend has some momentum. The distance between the buy point and the stop can be unduly large, as shown by arrow (X), which joins the buy at (A) to an initial stop at (B). In this case, it would have been greater than the moving average. This means, for this particular technique, *the parabolic should only be used to liquidate the second of our two units*; i.e., when the uptrend is already well established. In other words, once the oscillator has reached an extreme, it is the market's way of telling us the trend has accelerated sufficiently to increase the odds of a parabolic triggered stop being a timely one. Until that point, continue using the moving average as a triggering point, as before.

Setting Parabolic Parameters

There are two parameters that are required when plotting this indicator. The first parameter is the speed of the move and second, the maximum unit by which it can be increased. In Chart 10.7, the parabolic has been plotted as a .3 by a .3. This means that every time it is increased, the plot is raised (in an uptrend) by a factor of .3.

Chart 10.8 represents an enhanced view of rectangle (A) in Chart 10.7. The dashed line is a 30-period moving average and the solid line that crosses the price is the .3 times .3 parabolic. The 30-period price oscillator appears in the lower panel. The parabolic would be used in our two-unit approach in the following way: Initially the price slips below the moving average at (A), and a short position is opened. The first unit is covered as the oscillator reaches its oversold zone (B). The second part is covered when the price crosses above the parabolic line (C). As you can see, the parabolic covering signal was timelier, in this instance, than the signal of the moving average at (D).

Chart 10.9 features rectangle (A) of Chart 10.7. The moving average sell signal develops at (A). The first unit is covered early at (B), as the oscillator crosses its oversold zone. Then, the price slips some more, subsequently rallying above the parabolic at (C). Once again, the comparison with the regular moving average crossover, at (D), is favorable.

Chart 10.7   S&P Composite and 30-minute Close

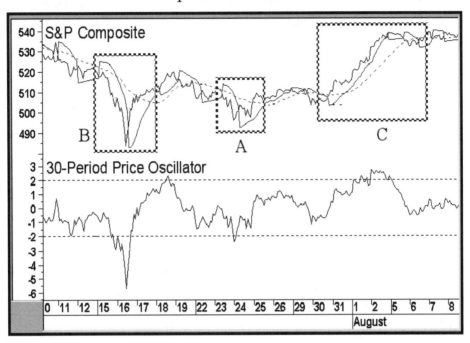

Chart 10.8   S&P Composite and 30-minute Close

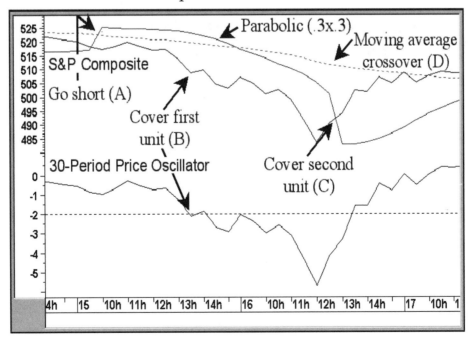

Finally, let us look at rectangle (C) in Chart 10.7. It is featured in Chart 10.10. The position is entered as the price crosses above its moving average at (A). The first unit is liquidated as the oscillator reaches its overbought level (B). Technically, it appears to have touched the overbought line earlier, so I may be overstretching the profit from this signal a bit. However, the liquidation of the second unit came on a timelier basis as the price slips below the parabolic line (C). Once again, the comparison of the two arrows shows that the parabolic was timelier than the moving average crossover, which developed at (D).

I am certainly not going to say that the parabolic will always work better than the moving average. This is certainly not the case in strong price trends, where prices go against the trend sufficiently to trigger a parabolic signal, but not a moving average crossover. In the vast majority of cases, though, I believe the parabolic will offer better exit signals than the moving average crossover. However, remember we are only executing parabolic signals after the oscillator has "done its thing" in registering an extreme reading; i.e., told us that the move has some underlying momentum.

Chart 10.9   S&P Composite and 30-minute Close

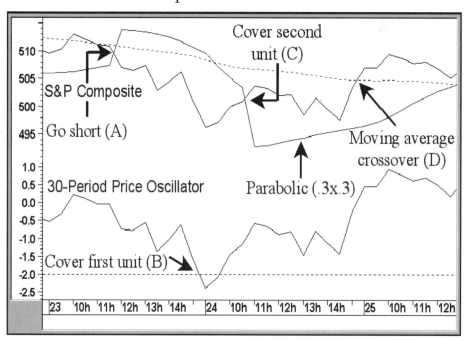

Chart 10.10 S&P Composite and 30-minute Close

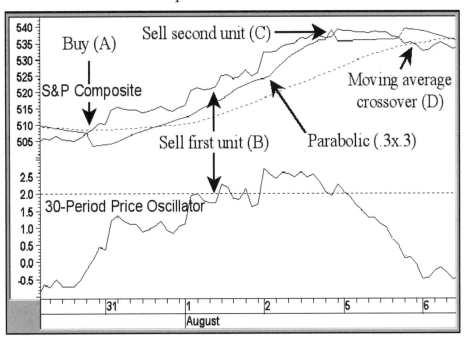

The RSI

I would like to close the discussion on this approach by introducing a 5-minute closing chart of the December 1998 NYSE Composite (Chart 10.11). In this instance, I have replaced the price oscillator with the more popular RSI (relative strength indicator). The time span, in this case, is 14 periods, or just over an hour. The moving average remains at 30 periods, as in the previous example. I started out by using a different span, but came back to 30 since it was the second best average, based on optimization. Testing covered spans from 10 to 80 periods. Actually, 28 periods came out slightly better than 30, but the difference was statistically insignificant. I took 30 because it is a round number. It also corresponds to 150 minutes or 2½ hours. I do not want to leave you with the idea that 30 is the best period for all securities using a 5-minute bar, because that is certainly not the case. I look upon 30 as a convenient, statistical triggering point for signals.

Overbought and oversold levels for the RSI are traditionally

Chart 10.11 NYSE Composite and 30-minute Close

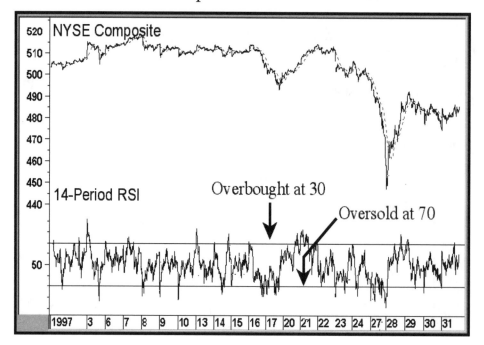

drawn at 70 and 30, as we see in Chart 10.11. However, after studying this price action a little more closely, I felt they should be
constructed using a wider band, since the 30 and 70 levels were
touched on numerous occasions. Consequently, in Chart 10.12,
they have been redrawn at 75 and 25. I have to admit that the
difference is not overwhelming, but the widening of the bands
limits the number of times when the RSI moves to an extreme
level—meaning profits are allowed to run a little more.

Chart 10.13 shows a specific period of the previous one in more
detail. The parabolic curve, once again, is shown as the solid line
that is continually crossing above and below the price. This time,
I changed the parameters from .2 and .3 to .02 and .10. By reducing the maximum movement factor, the indicator becomes less
sensitive. I thought this necessary in view of the greater level of
volatility in the 5-minute chart for any given time span, than the
volatility of the 30-minute chart we were studying earlier.

The price action starts off with a short signal at (A), as the price
crosses below the 30-period moving average. The initial unit is
covered at (A_1), as the RSI falls to its 25-oversold zone for a nice

Chart 10.12 NYSE Composite and 5-minute Bar

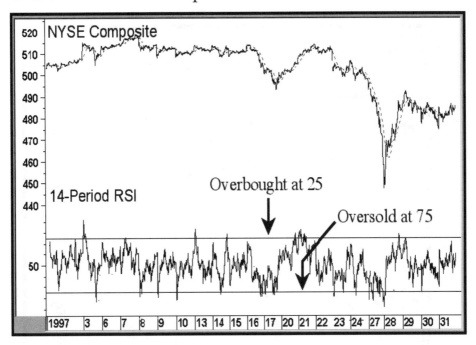

profit. The second unit is covered, a little bit later, as the price rallies above the parabolic at (A_2). This was an improvement on the moving average crossover, which developed a little higher at (A_3). The next signal associated with a RSI overbought/oversold crossover came at (B). The oscillator rallied up to the 75 level and the first unit was liquidated at (B_1), again, for a small profit. Finally, the price falls, the parabolic rises, and the second unit is liquidated at (B_2). The moving average crossover developed a little later at (B_3), but, again, at a less profitable level than the parabolic.

So far, we have seen that, in most cases, the parabolic signal beats the moving average crossover, but not by much. This appears to be true for the vast majority of signals. In some respect, we could say that the parabolic is scalping profits from the moving average.

However, when we get an unusually persistent trend, the tide is turned the other way. Chart 10.14 shows such an example. An initial short position is executed as the price breaks below its average at (A). The RSI quickly moves to an oversold condition and

Chart 10.13 NYSE Composite and 5-minute Bar

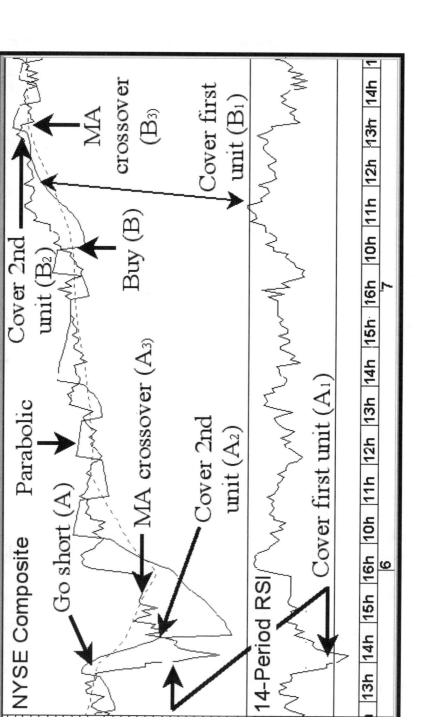

the first unit is covered at (A₁). Not long after, it moves below the parabolic (A₂) and the position is now flat. Unfortunately, this was way too premature since the price continued falling until the moving average crossover at (A₃). The vertical distance between the two signals shows how much profit was given up by liquidating on the parabolic signal. We have to remember that this kind of persistent trend is extremely unusual. I suppose we could have used the next sell signal in the parabolic at (B) to get back in. However, even at this point, there was a whipsaw and another brief trading range before the final plunge. Just how unusual this trend was can be seen from Chart 10.15. This is a daily chart covering all of 1997. There is nothing that comes close to this comparison with the Asian financial collapse/decline.

We have to remember that trading the markets is a question of taking profits while we can, and cutting losses. It would be nice to maximize profits, but that is not possible. Most of the time, the parabolic/momentum concept works well. Even in the example shown, both positions made money and, indeed, they needed to because I have totally ignored the many whipsaws that develop

Chart 10.14 NYSE Composite and 5-minute Bar

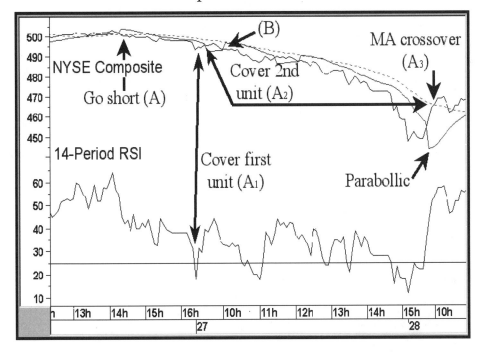

with moving average crossovers. As you can now appreciate, the concept of taking profits on an overbought or oversold reading is really done to pay for a substantial number of small losses generated from many whipsaw signals. ∎

Chart 10.15 S&P Composite and 5-minute Bar

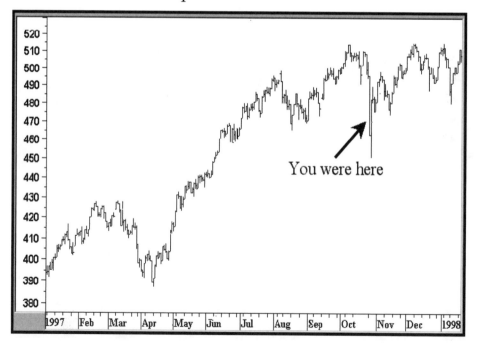

Chapter 11

The KST System
in Real Time

The Importance of Time Frames

I mentioned in the chapter on trends that when trading or investing in any time frame it is important to have an understanding of the direction of the main trend. On the daily or weekly charts, the main or primary trend lasts from one to two years. To briefly recap, it is represented in Figure 11.1 by the thick line. The intermediate trend, lasting anywhere from 6 weeks to 9 months, and short-term trend that develops over a two to six week horizon, are also labeled. The short-term trend is very much influenced by the primary trend. The magnitude of a move is greater when in concert with the primary trend. Thus, short-term rallies are stronger in a primary bull market as are the declines in a bear market. If a problem interpreting the charts is going to arise, it will usually show up then because you are positioning yourself on a short-term signal that develops in a contrary direction to the main trend. In effect, you are trading upstream when the river is flowing downstream. You can paddle upstream and it is possible to

Figure 11.1 Market Cycle Model

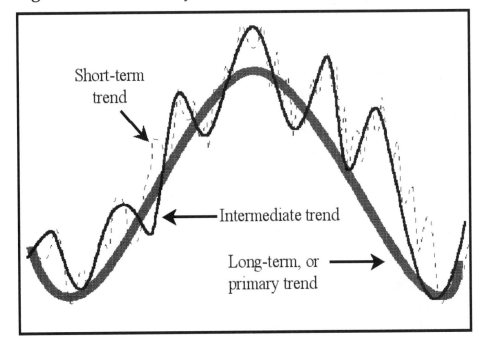

make money going against the main trend; however, both are far more difficult.

You may be wondering why this is important for intraday trading when the time frames are so much shorter. Well, the same principle applies to intraday trading in that the direction and magnitude of short-term trends influences the characteristics of intraday price swings. Consequently, it is important for the intraday trader to have some idea of the direction of the short-term trend. Just as a rising primary trend lifts all boats for an investor, so a rising short-term trend has the same effect for the intraday trader. With traditional charts we really have only two data possibilities for short-term trends, daily and weekly, and normally we would work with daily bars. However, with intraday charts there is a whole range of possibilities starting with tick, working through a minute, 5, 10, 15, and 30 minute all the way to hourly charts. This makes things a bit more complicated, but not an impossible problem to solve, especially if we realize that technical analysis should never be regarded as a precise scientific technique but more of a free flowing common sense art form.

Learning to Identify Dominant Intraday Trends

The questions we need to answer are: what is the time frame of the main trend? And secondly, what is the best way to identify reversals? The answer to the first question will depend on the periodicity of the chart we are monitoring. If it is a tick chart, the time frame will be much shorter than a 30-minute bar. Many technical analysts use moving averages to smooth out a trend, and use the position of the price relative to the average to determine the trend's direction. I personally prefer to use a smoothed momentum measure, often in conjunction with a moving average, or some other form of trend reversal identification technique. Changes in the direction of the smoothed momentum, as signaled with a moving average crossover, offer a framework to identify important trend reversals, such as, the buy signal at (A) in Chart 11.1, and the sell signal at (B). In this way, reversals in the momentum signal a change in trend. Oscillators also provide us with another dimension—the

Chart 11.1   September 1997 US Treasury Bonds

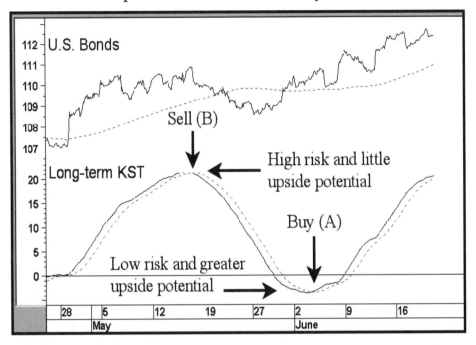

maturity of the trend. At (A), the indicator is very overbought and, based on statistical averages, the risk is outweighed by any potential reward. On the other hand, an oscillator that has just reversed direction from well below zero, or the equilibrium line, tells us that the emerging bull trend has plenty of upside potential. The reversal at (A) is just a little bit below zero, but the indicator can still run quite a way before becoming overextended.

Having established these principles, it is now necessary to choose a suitable oscillator. My choice is the **KST** (**K**now **S**ure **T**hing), a smoothed momentum indicator that I originally developed for standard daily, weekly and monthly charts. The formulas for the KST are reproduced in the Appendix and an area is also available on the CD for copying into your MetaStock® program. If your software does not have the flexibility to allow you to program in the KST, do not lose heart since there is no reason why you cannot adapt time frames from other smoothed oscillators such as the Stochastics or the Price Oscillator. The principles I am going to outline are common to them all but first, a few words on the concept behind the KST's construction.

The Concept Behind the KST

Price, at any one time, is determined by the interaction of many different time cycles. When we look at an oscillator with a specific time frame, we are only privy to one of those cycles. Therefore, it makes sense to consider several oscillators based on different time frames. We will never get a complete picture because there are far too many cycles to monitor—but we will certainly achieve a more comprehensive one. The **KST construction** takes this into consideration since it is based on four different rates of change time frames. Each time frame is then smoothed by a moving average and combined into one indicator. I should also add that each smoothed ROC is weighted, the longest span getting the highest weighting, and so forth. The weighting process is important because we want the longest time frame to dominate and, therefore, reflect the major swings. The shorter time frames help to make the KST more sensitive. Thus, we have a good compromise between timeliness and sensitivity; i.e., whipsaws are kept to a minimum, but signals are relatively timely. KSTs can be designed for any time frame from short-term daily trends to long-term monthly ones. If you would like to learn more about the KST, there is a CD ROM tutorial on the subject complete with a quiz. More information can be found in the back of this book. I can sow the seed here, but barely scratch the surface.

Chart 11.2 features December 1997 corn, and contains an example of a 15-minute bar KST. Momentum buy and sell signals are given when the KST crosses above and below its moving average. The average, in this instance, is based on a 10-period, or 2½ hour time frame. The sharp uptrend between the 6th and 13th offered two buy signals, but each developed when the KST was at a very overextended level. The signals were followed by very worthwhile rallies. Usually, it is better to ignore them when they are triggered from such a high level since the odds are against you. The next buy signal (early on the 15th) came from a lower level, but was followed by a sideways move. However, the buy signal on the morning of the 20th did develop from a low level, and was followed by a very worthwhile advance. As time progresses, you can see that the buy signals lost money or barely broke even, whereas, the sell signals would have made a small profit by going

Chart 11.2   December 1997 Corn 15-minute Bar

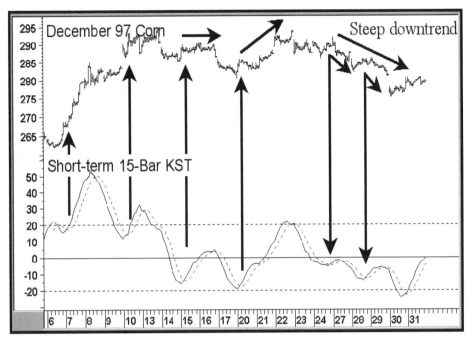

short. In retrospect, it is easy to see why, because the price was in a sharp downtrend. At the time, though, we could not have known the steepness of the decline, but there are some techniques that could have provided a clue as to the direction of the trend. That is where our KST, based on longer-term time frames, comes in. This is covered in the next section.

Integrating the Short- and Long-term KSTs

Chart 11.3 reveals four principal trends: two up, and two down. These are also reflected in three of the swings of the long-term KST. (The moving average for the long-term KST is an 80-period or 20-hour time frame.) You may notice that the KST is sometimes very timely, like the sell signal at (A), but it also is sometimes late, like the signal at (B). In very strong markets, the KST will turn down prematurely, well ahead of the price. Clearly, it is not

a perfect indicator, but it does give us a reference point to base
our trading decisions on. If you look at the short-term buy signals when the long-term KST is in a declining trend, you can see
that most of them were of very poor magnitude. The exception
was the one on the 20th.   However, this was the start of a bull
trend. Regrettably, the long-term KST had not yet picked up that
point, so the emerging trend was not apparent. As we move on, I
will discuss techniques for anticipating some of these characteristics. Unfortunately, we do not have any short-term buy signals
for those periods when the long-term KST was rising. I have highlighted the two signals on the left, however (X_1 and X_2). Even
though we do not have the data, it was quite clear from the level
of the long-term KST when it peaked, that these signals developed when the KST was rising. Unfortunately, this chart does not
demonstrate many sell signals in a bullish environment—apart
from those three on the extreme left where the lack of data does
not enable us to see the rising long-term KST.

Chart 11.4 features a 5-minute bar of the September 1997 S&P
Futures. Two of the three sell signals in the bullish trend (A_1 and
A_2) did not pan out. The third, in the ellipse, did. This is because
it marked the actual peak for the rally. Since the time span for a 5-
minute bar is different from the 15-minute bar which we were
looking at earlier, so are the time spans used in the KST construction. I am not going to say these are the best combinations; the
important point is that this combination appears to work *reasonably* well <u>most of the time</u>.

I do not want to give you the impression that all contra-trend
short-term KST signals offer no magnitude whatsoever, for that is
certainly not the case. In Chart 11.5, I have flagged the KST
uptrends with the dashed arrow. Look at the smaller downward
pointing arrows denoting sell signals. They do not result in cata-
strophic declines, but each is followed by a sideways correction
or small down move. The conclusion is that the effect of a signal
very much depends on the nature of the long-term trend. If it is
relatively modest, the sell signals will offer some respite from the
advance. On the other hand, if the trend is stronger, then the sell
signals are probably not going to amount to very much. For the
most part, you can see that the short-term signals, which go in
sympathy with the main trend (as defined by the long-term KST)
offer good magnitude. Conversely, if things are going to go wrong,

Chart 11.3 December 1997 Corn 15-minute Bar

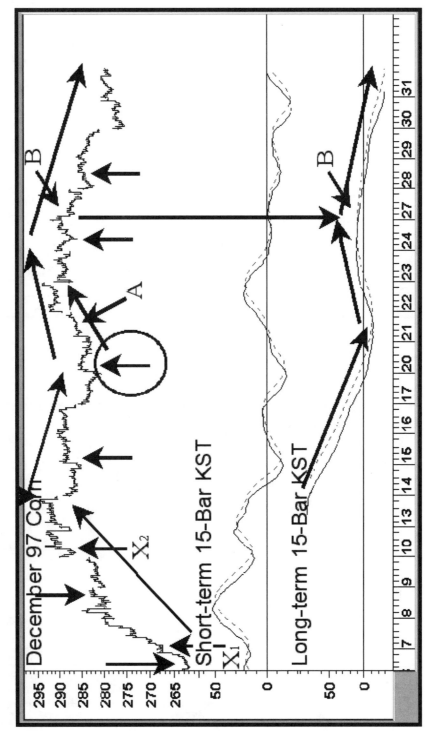

Chart 11.4   September 1997 S&P Composite 5-minute Bar

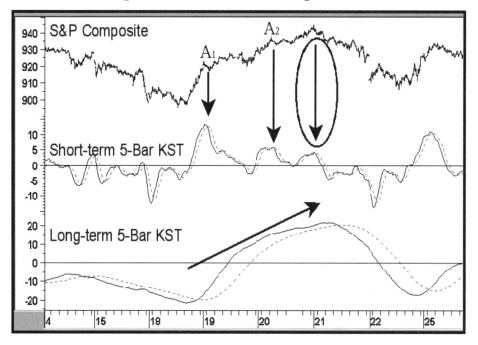

Chart 11.5   September 1997 S&P Composite 5-minute Bar

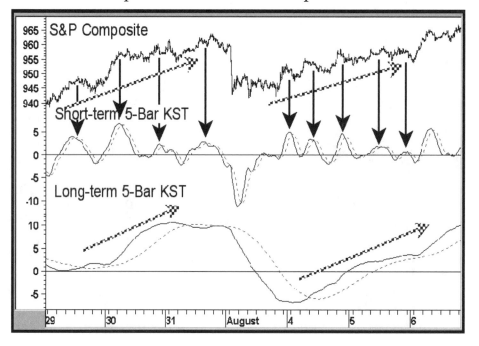

it will invariably happen when the signal develops in the opposite direction of the long-term series. But how do we know when a specific short-term signal actually represents the first near-term price movement in a new long-term trend? After all, the long-term KST normally lags major turning points so these signals appear to develop in a counter-cyclical way. We only know *for sure* with the benefit of hindsight. Price action in the markets often provides a clue, but there are some pointers we can look for.

Anticipating Long-term KST Reversals

In Chart 11.6 we see a strong short-term KST buy signal that develops in what appears to be a downtrend. First of all, it is important to observe the position and slope of the long-term KST. If it is very overextended, it is quite possible that the next contra-trend signal will actually turn out to be the first pro-trend signal in a new trend. In this instance the KST is around zero at the time of the reversal. At the time the short-term buy signal is triggered, the KST has begun to flatten out, but it is still below its moving average. The flattening provides us with some evidence that if the buy signal results in a rally, there will not be sufficient downside momentum to enable the long-term KST to decline. The short-term signal places us on alert for this possibility. The next thing to watch out for is a rally above trendline (A), because it represents important resistance. When the price does violate the line, it signals that a series of rising peaks and troughs is now underway. It also, simultaneously, violates a down trendline (B). So, from the price aspect, we have three pieces of evidence that the trend has reversed: the two trendline violations and the peak and trough reversal. This is sufficient evidence to conclude that the downside momentum in the long-term KST has been reversed. In this particular instance, the KST crosses its average just a little bit after the price trend break takes place. The reversal is often delayed for much longer than this because it usually takes quite a bit of price action to affect the long-term KST. In this instance, the signal was very timely, but certainly not profitable since the price soon began to reverse trend again.

Now let us take a closer look at the sell signal on the 27th in Chart 11.7. First of all, the KST had already begun to roll over, so

Chart 11.6   December 1997 Corn 15-minute Bar

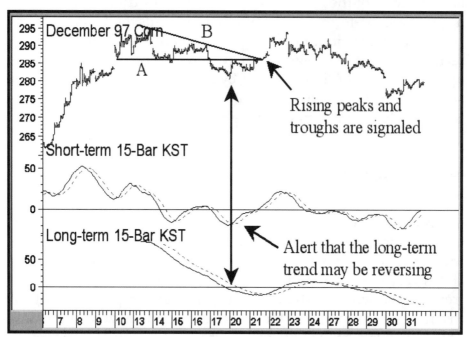

unless a sharp rally is signaled, the odds favored a sell signal. That was unlikely to happen because the price had previously violated an important up trendline. There were two possible implications from this: 1) either a reversal to the downside, or 2) an extended sideways trend. Neither outcome argued for a strong long-term KST. Second, the short-term KST gave a sell signal, but look where it came from. In this instance, the KST was barely above zero. This type of action, when confirmed by a price trend break, is often followed by a pretty nasty decline. It was not too bad in this case, but this weak momentum syndrome has preceded some of the worst I have ever seen.   Finally, the price completes a top and breaks down. This was the coup de grace for the long-term KST.

One other point before we leave this chart, relates to the potential power of a short-term KST signal. Most signals do not give us much of a clue as to the magnitude of the ensuing move. However, if a trendline can be constructed for the KST and it is violated, it emphasizes the strength of the signal. In effect, this particular signal could well reverse or interrupt a whole trend of previous short-term signals. In Chart 11.7, (C) is a declining

Chart 11.7   December 1997 S&P 15-minute Bar

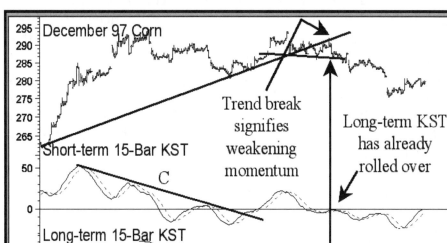

trendline, which is quickly penetrated just after the final short-term buy. This represented powerful evidence that downside momentum had been dealt a severe blow, and that a reversal in the long-term KST was very likely.

If we look at Chart 11.8, we can see a break in KST trendline (A) that preceded the long-term reversal, again a very powerful message that downside momentum was probably exhausted. This was later confirmed by a small trendline violation in the price (C). Finally, a larger trendline (B) was successfully penetrated.

Now to study the next long-term reversal to the upside: First, the short-term KST trendline (D) was violated. Actually, if you look carefully, you will see that the KST also formed and broke out from a reverse head and shoulders pattern. Then, a small price trendline (E) was violated. Finally, a longer-term line (F) was penetrated just before the KST crossed its moving average.

Let us now turn our attention to the long-term KST sell signal in Chart 11.9. First of all, notice that the KST is, unlike our previous examples, quite overextended. This means that in order to keep rising and remain in bullish territory it must continue to receive larger and larger doses of higher prices. As time moves on, you can see that upside momentum, preceding the peak in the long-term KST was definitely dissipating. Evidence in this direction comes from the declining peaks in the short-term KST that accompanied the higher peaks in the price. Finally, these negative divergences were confirmed by the price itself, which violated an important up trendline (A). Actually, this was confirming what had previously happened with the short-term KST, which had also violated a major up trendline (B). Note how the line was great support prior to its violation. Once the extended line was penetrated, it took on the role of resistance, as the short-term KST rally was unable to seriously break back above it. Finally, the price completes and breaks down from a head and shoulders top. This gives us sufficient warning to not participate in the long side, since it indicated that the strong uptrend was over.

Chart 11.8   September 1997 S&P 5-minute Bar

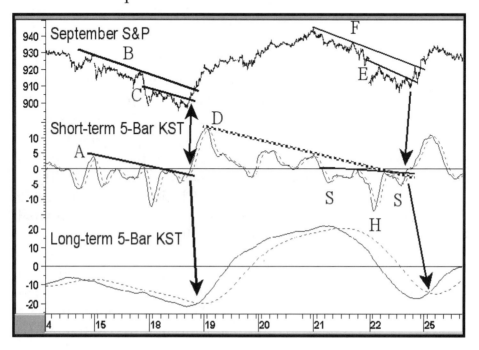

Chart 11.9   September 1997 S&P 5-minute Bar

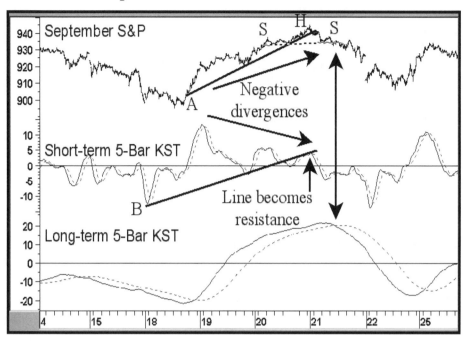

The KST Using Tick Data

Finally, an example of a short-term KST based on tick data is shown in Chart 11.10. Because tick charts are so jagged and almost random in nature, I find the best way to use the KST is to again revert to the overbought/oversold analysis. In this example, I have placed the overbought/oversold lines at plus and minus four. The best signals on tick charts appear to come when the KST reaches an extreme, and then reverses direction, rather than waiting for a return crossover on the way to the equilibrium line. You must also remember that we are dealing with tick data, where time is of the essence. The ability to react to technical developments has to be almost instantaneous. Otherwise, the new trend will be well underway before the order can be placed and executed. Chart 11.12 magnifies part of Chart 11.11 so we can take a look at the KST in closer detail. Most of the time, the KST reaches the overbought/oversold extreme and reverses direction, as does the price. The downward pointing arrows reflect the sell signals. In

Chart 11.10 December 1997 S&P 5-minute Bar

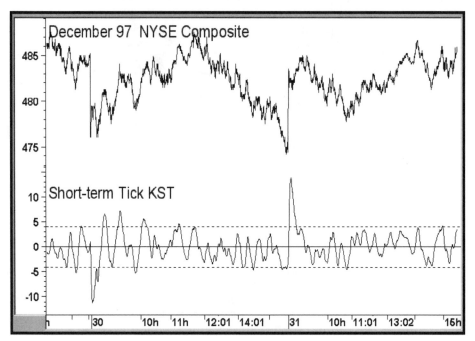

most cases, they are very timely. Waiting for the return crossover in most situations means a later signal. The vertical dashed lines show the actual KST peaks. As you can see, in most instances, they offer a timelier sell signal than the overbought crossover. This means that as soon as you realize the KST has peaked from an extreme level, it is time to place an order to sell. Chart 11.12 shows the same period, but this time the buy signals have been flagged. You can see they are just as timely. Again, it often makes sense to buy, or cover, a short position as soon as you realize that the KST has troughed from an extreme level. Several signals do not have lines because the KST really just touched the oversold line and bounced. However, there was one bad signal, which I have highlighted with the letter (A). It was far too premature and is a stark reminder that wherever possible, it is always best to have a momentum signal confirmed by a price trend reversal signal. In this case, a good place to put a stop would have been below the minor low indicated by the arrow (B).

Chart 11.11   December 1997 NYSE Composite Tick

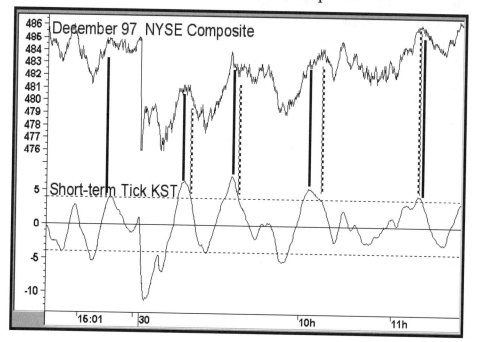

Chart 11.12   December 1997 NYSE Composite Tick

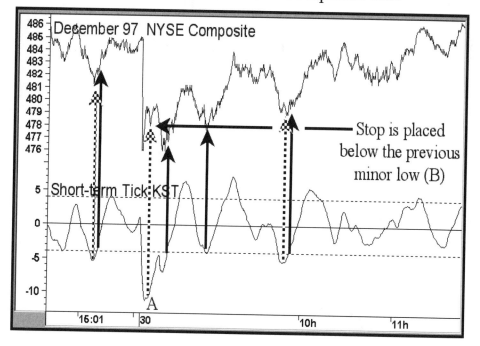

On the whole, the signals in these tick charts were pretty good. However, it is important to remember that there is no way anyone can consistently sell at the high and buy on the low. Both the premature buy and the premature sell would have resulted in very satisfactory exit points, both on the short and long sides.

I am sure you will agree, there are many ways the KST can be integrated into analysis. I have only scratched the surface here with this brief introduction. ■

Chapter 12

Bollinger Bands

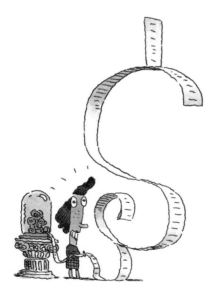

The Concept

Technical analysts have traditionally drawn **envelopes** above and below moving averages in an attempt to capture the overbought and oversold conditions as an alternative to the oscillator concept. Chart 12.1 shows a 25-bar simple moving average (A) with two other smooth series featured. The lower series (B) is a 25-bar average plotted 1% below the actual average and (C) is plotted 1% above it. The idea is that a correctly drawn envelope will offer good dynamic areas of support and resistance. It is really another way of looking at a price oscillator, which is calculated as a deviation from the trend. In Chart 12.2, the price oscillator is calculated by dividing the daily close by a 25-day moving average. You can see that the +1% overbought level is exactly the same as the price touching the upper envelope, because the envelope is plotted 1% above the average. Similarly, the oversold line corresponds to the price touching the lower envelope.

Chart 12.1   June 1997 S&P Composite 15-minute Bar

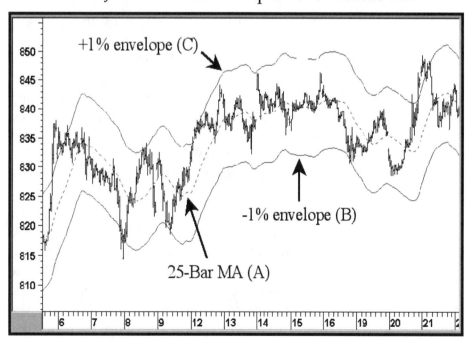

Chart 12.2   June 1997 S&P Composite 15-minute Bar

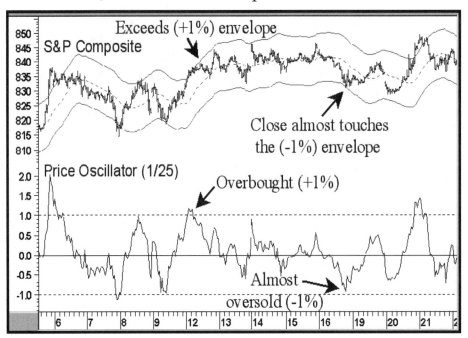

Bollinger Bands (Chart 12.3) operate in a similar way, except that the envelopes, or bands, are calculated using standard deviations. For those of you who, like me, are not mathematically oriented, a simple explanation is that the bands contract or expand depending on the level of volatility. The greater the volatility, the wider the bands and vice versa. The first requirement in plotting a Bollinger Band is a time span, as you would a moving average. The longer the span, the smoother, but less sensitive are the fluctuations. The upper band in Chart 12.4 is a 65-bar span, whereas the lower one is a 10-bar span. It is pretty obvious that the 65-bar span is far smoother and is plotted further away from the price action.

The second parameter for plotting a Bollinger Band is the amount of deviation. In this respect, the bands in Chart 12.5 are calculated with a deviation of one. This results in a very tight band, which is touched so many times it is not useful. On the other hand, a larger deviation factor returns a band that is a long way from the price and is rarely, if ever, touched. Think of the deviation as a parameter that corresponds with an overbought/

Chart 12.3   December 1997 NYSE Composite
20/2 Bollinger Band

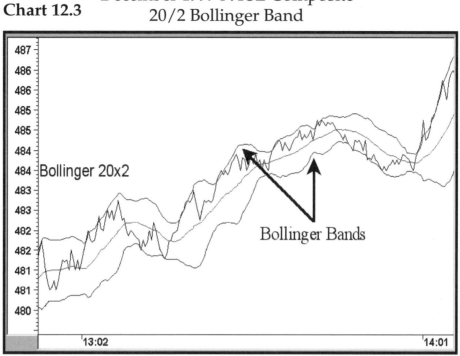

Chart 12.4   June 1997 S&P Composite 15-minute Bar

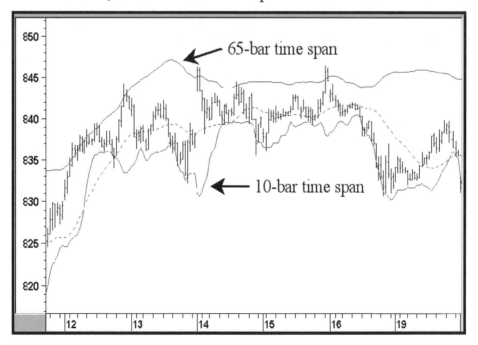

Chart 12.5   December 1997 S&P Composite 30-minute Bar

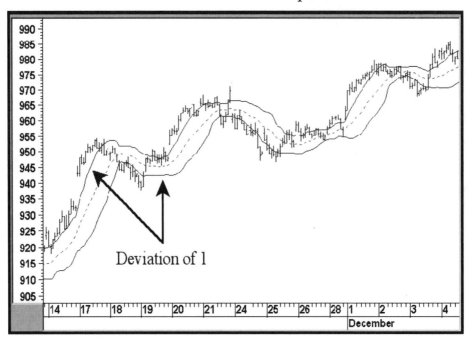

oversold level. Chart 12.6 is an example using a deviation of five showing that the bands are rarely, if ever, touched by the price. In this instance, the bands are useless as an analytical device. It is like drawing an overbought/oversold combination that is never touched. As with overbought/oversold zones, the chosen level will depend on the time span and the degree of volatility inherent to the security being monitored. John Bollinger, the creator of this technique, recommends a factor of 20 for the time span and two for the deviation.

Chart 12.6 December 1997 S&P Composite 30-minute Bar

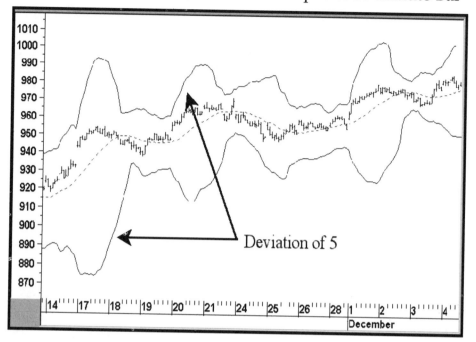

Deviation of 5

Rules for Interpretation

There are several rules for interpreting the bands:

Rule 1. When the bands narrow, there is a tendency for sharp price changes to follow.

In this context, a narrowing of the band is always relative to the recent past. In Chart 12.7, a tick chart featuring the NYSE Composite, you can see that the bands come very close together (at A), and this is later followed by a good move to the upside. I put in several trendlines (C) so it becomes more apparent that this was a trading range. In situations like this, the narrowing of the bands is the same thing as saying that a period of consolidation that is followed by a breakout will experience a good trend. However, the bands do give us some indication of when a breakout might materialize because they start to diverge once the price begins to take off. In other situations, a trading range is not so

Chart 12.7   December 1997 NYSE Composite Tick

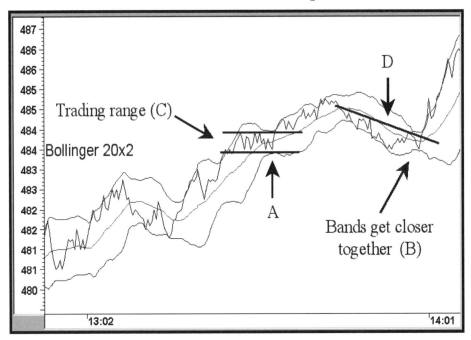

evident. Take the example of the narrowing that took place at (B) a little later on. The bands tightened, but there was no apparent place where two trendlines, marking a trading range, could be constructed. However, it was possible to construct a down trendline. Its penetration, along with the narrowing of the bands, signaled a very nice rally.

> **Rule 2.** If the price exceeds a band, the trend is expected to continue.

This is really another way of saying that if the price moves above the band, upside momentum is strong enough to support higher ultimate prices and vice versa. In Chart 12.8 at (A) you can see that the price experiences a trading range and then breaks to the downside. The signal that the trend will continue comes from the point where the price exceeds the band on the downside. It then rallies back a bit and continues to zig-zag down. Later on, it experiences a trading range (B) and eventually breaks to the downside. Once again, the drop below the lower band indicated by the

Chart 12.8   December 1997 S&P Composite 5-minute Bar

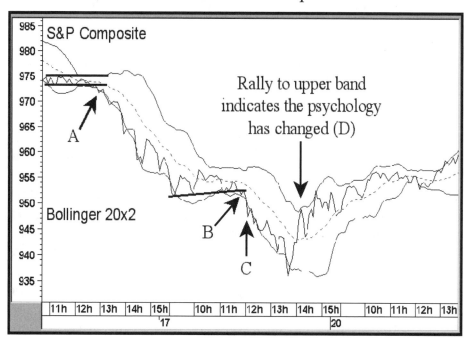

arrow at (C), is the signal that prices are headed lower. Finally, the price breaks below the lower band again and then immediately rallies back to the upper line (D), indicating the trend will continue, but now we are looking at an uptrend. When you think of it, it is the first time in the history of the chart that there was a rally to the upper band, indicating a definite switch in psychology from the bearish to the bullish side. As you can see, the uptrend continued for a while. So, when you see a price break above the upper band or below the lower band following a trading range, or a sharp decline or rally, it is a signal that the price probably has sufficient momentum for the trend to continue. The crossover of the Bollinger Band usually indicates short-term exhaustion and it quickly pulls back again. However, this is just a pause for breath until the trend is then able to extend again.

By now you will have noticed that the price often crosses the bands several times before the trend reverses. The obvious question at this point is: How do you know when the band has been crossed for the last time? In other words how do you know how to spot the bottom and top of a move? The answer lies in Rule 3.

Rule 3. When the price traces out a reversal formation after it has crossed outside a band, expect a trend reversal.

In Chart 12.9 we see a series of three rallies that touch or exceed the upper band (A). The first two show no sign of exhaustion. However, after the final attempt, the up trendline is violated. Then the price falls below the previous minor low to complete a small top at (F).

Later, the price touches the outer band again at (B), but there is no signal since it manages to hold above the lower portion of the trading range. There are no signals at (D) following subsequent upper band penetrations. Finally, a nice up trendline is violated, and a sell signal is triggered (E). What we are literally seeing is a series of overbought readings—that is what a price touching the band really is. It finally confirms the overbought reading. If there is no signal, the implication is that following a brief correction, the price will then go on to register a new high or low for the move, depending on its direction. That is not always the case, because there is no such word as "always" when working with

Chart 12.9   December 1997 NYSE Composite Tick

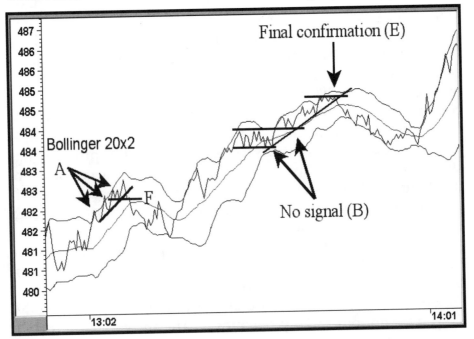

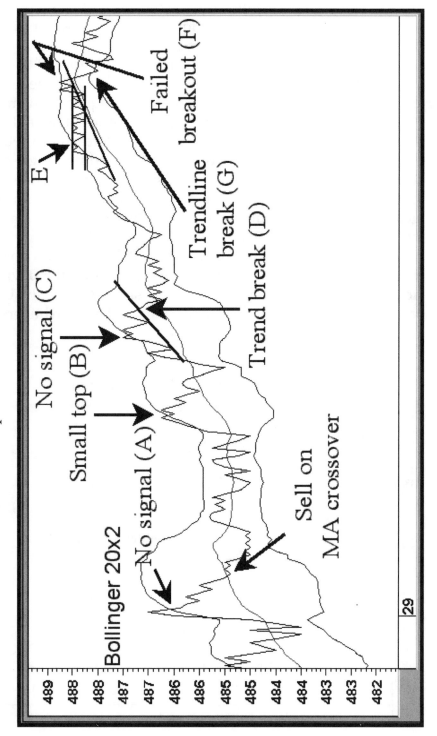

Chart 12.10 December 1997 NYSE Composite Tick

technical indicators. For instance, Chart 12.10 shows where the price crosses below the upper band (A), yet, it does not go on to make a new high until a worthwhile decline had taken place. In such instances, the best place to liquidate a long position is when the price crosses below the moving average.

Later on, at (B), you can see a small double top, as the price tries for a second time to break above the band. At the next attempt (C) there is no signal, but after the subsequent penetration, a trendline is violated (D). Then, we see a series of lows (E), but this support was not broken so there was no reason to sell. Finally, the price tries to break out from the trading range, but is held back by the upper band (F). A subsequent trendline break (G) is the signal to liquidate. In retrospect, what we see is a failed breakout, which just adds to the bearishness once the series of lows is penetrated on the downside.

Sometimes it is possible to combine Bollinger Band analysis with the KST. In Chart 12.11 we have expanded the deviation factor from 2 to 2.5 with a 25-bar time span. At (A), the bands narrow appreciably, indicating a fine balance between buyers and

Chart 12.11 December 1998 Bonds 15-minute Bar

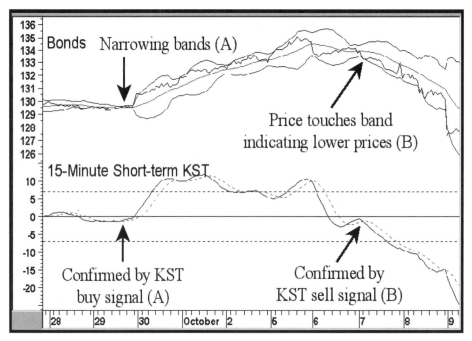

sellers. The question is: Which way will the price break? A vital clue can sometimes be gleaned by looking at an oscillator. In this chart, I am using the KST, but it could easily be the MACD, Stochastic, RSI and so forth. The idea is that the KST has just triggered a buy signal, just a few moments before the price exploded to the upside. A little later (B), the bands narrow and the price breaks to the lower band. This move to the lower band indicated that prices were likely to decline. Stronger evidence in this direction was provided by the KST, which had already signaled a sell signal. ∎

Chapter 13

Where and Where *Not* to Place Stops

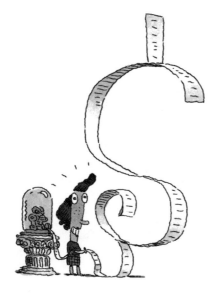

Advantages and Disadvantages of Setting Stops

Setting **protective stops** is an essential ingredient in any leveraged trading activity. This process can either be done physically, by actually placing them in advance with your broker, or you can decide mentally where a stop should be executed. If a stop is placed physically, it may involve setting an alert with your software and watching the price action very closely. On the other hand, if you set the stop mentally, you may be focusing on one specific market, and can immediately execute an order the moment the stop is reached. It does not really matter. The advantage of having the stop in the market is that it will be executed immediately, and there is no second-guessing. The disadvantage of a physical stop is that market makers and locals can see your stops and may try to "go" for them. The disadvantage of placing a mental stop is that you may change your mind for the wrong reason when the price reaches that particular level. This could be induced by fear of taking a loss, or just wanting to give the price a little more room. For either reason, the change of mind is triggered under the duress of market action rather than objective thinking. Unless you are sure this will not happen and that you will stick to your guns, the mental stop approach is not advisable. Whichever method you use, the important point is to make sure, when you enter a trade, you know exactly where you are going to get out if things go against you. As time progresses and prices change, the level of the stop is also altered. If you are trading more than one contract, or several hundred shares, there is no reason why you cannot split the stop at different price levels. After all, we are dealing with probabilities, and if the probabilities are not so great, exposure should be less.

There are several advantages to placing stops. First, by the very nature of establishing a stop level that is either physically or mentally entered, you are going through the mental process of preparing yourself for the worst. In the case of profit-taking stops, it will be a mental preparation of an optimistic outcome.

Quite often, when prices go against you, your emotions become clouded, making an objective decision harder to accomplish.

Placing the stop helps to overcome this problem since the decision to do so will be made when your mind is more equally balanced. If prices move sharply in your direction, it is often accompanied by good news, so good in fact that it is easy to fall into the trap of believing that the price will continue to trend forever. That, unfortunately, is often the point when the price will reach an extreme.

Another advantage is that a correctly placed stop will usually get you out at a better price than just throwing in a market order. This is because a stop order is executed as a market order, once the stipulated price has been touched. If you are just watching the market and suddenly decide to stop yourself out, it is quite possible that the time delay will result in a far worse fill. My comments here assume that the stop is executed in a reasonably orderly market. In some instances, when dramatic news such as an unexpected economic report breaks, there is literally no liquidity even in the most "liquid" markets. In such an environment, orders can be executed at levels that would emit four letter words from even the most docile traders.

Placing Stops

With long positions, the best and most obvious point to place a **sell stop** is just below support or for covering a short position above resistance. The terms support and resistance in this sense, can mean a lot of things. Support, in reference to stops for instance, may develop at a specified price level. Alternatively, it could be dynamic in the sense of a trendline or moving average acting as a support level. The key is to place a stop just *below* support not *at* it. After all, if the price does not slip below a support level, or rise above a resistance level, the trend is not reconfirmed or reversed, depending on the circumstances.

Chart 13.1 is a 45-period moving average and the bars are 10 minutes in length for the corn contract. It features an example of a top forming. Had we placed the stop at the trendline; i.e., at support, the stop would have been triggered and the trade would not have gone on to make a good profit. It would have been far better to place it below support as indicated by line (B) and the moving average, since the two re-enforce themselves as support areas. Signals, as a result of a trendline and moving average viola-

Chart 13.1   December 1997 Corn 10-minute Bar

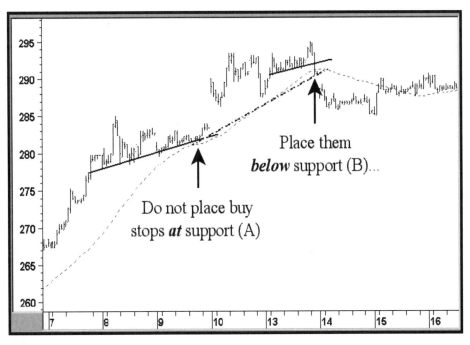

tion, are generally far more significant than those that only penetrate one of them. **Buy stops** should be placed *above* resistance.
In Chart 13.2 we see a resistance trendline (A), which is really a
neckline of a consolidating reverse head and shoulders. This
would, subject to the agreement of our momentum analysis, be a
legitimate place to make a purchase. However, within 20 minutes the price broke down again, as the breakout was false (B).
We would have expected the neckline to hold, since it has now
reversed its role to support following the breakout. Its penetration was the first sign of trouble. However, once the price slipped
below the trendline joining the lows forming the right shoulder
(C), it was the signal to liquidate. As you can see, the bar, during
which this took place, started 20 minutes before the session close.
The damage was pretty well done in 10 minutes. Consequently,
there was not a lot of time to react. It would have been far better
to place the stop just below the trendline (D) (support) in advance,
because by the time the bar ended the price was also below the
moving average. The next day, of course, it gapped down at the
opening (E).

Chart 13.2   December 1997 Corn 10-minute Bar

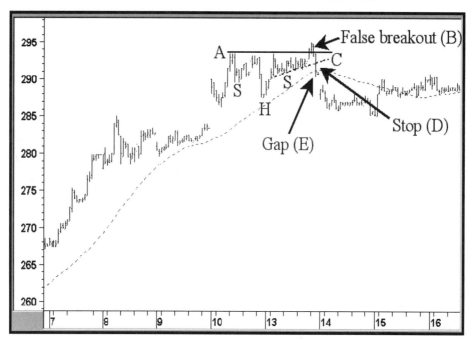

Timely stops can also be placed for getting into positions following breakouts. Chart 13.3 features a breakout, which is quickly followed by a pullback. The retracement takes it right back to the breakout level. This was previously a point of resistance, but now reverses its role to support. Consequently, it would have made sense to place a buy stop as the price was falling back to that support level. If the support was seriously violated, the position could have been quickly liquidated for a nominal loss.

Chart 13.3 also offers an example of a good place to exit a position, or part of a position, by placing a stop at the previous high. (This is the lower end where the 13:30 gap formed on the 29th and this also represents resistance.)   Let us say we had been lucky enough to go short at (X). This level would have represented a great point to place a stop from the point of view of covering the position. It is not a great point, though, because it was not only close to a break even level, but because a stop above this high would have represented excellent resistance. As it turned out, the price never broke above this significant resistance level, so the short position ended the chart with a small profit.

Chart 13.3   December 1997 Corn 10-minute Bar

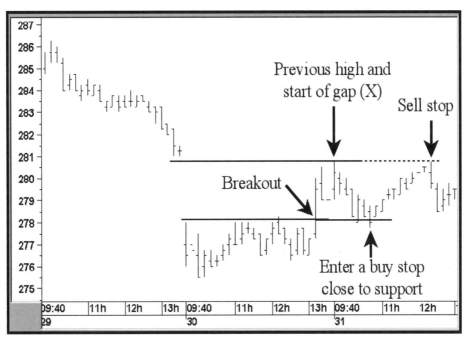

Using Extreme Bars to Place Stops

The extreme points of highly emotional bars often represent good support and resistance zones, and therefore good points to place stops. Chart 13.4 shows an example of an **extreme bar** at (A). The price rallies, so we know that support exists around the low of the extreme bar, although, in this case, the rally is too far advanced to allow a good risk/reward trade. The price then falls back again, but does not take out the extreme low. Finally, it does penetrate our support level on its way to a serious new low. Note that the bar containing the support violating low is an extreme bar in its own right. It, too, acts as a support level, as you can see from trendline (X). One more point before we leave this chart. The start of the gap on the left represented a great support level, as the gap was being closed. It is important to remember that these emotional bar extremes only represent short-term support and resistance points. They are very useful for trading purposes during the next 20 to 30 bars, but not much else. ■

Chart 13.4   June 1997 Bonds 15-minute Bar

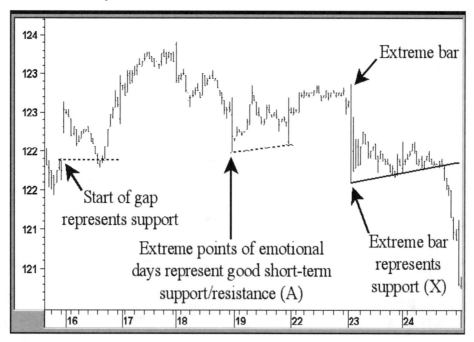

Chapter 14

Street Smart
Trading Tips

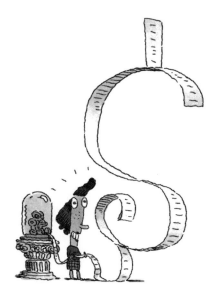

Go With the Leader

During the trading session, many things are going on under the surface. Some stocks are leading, others are lagging. The same is true in the commodity pits. Gold and silver, for instance, are closely related, but usually there is a leader and a laggard. It pays to find out which is the leader because this will, typically, offer advance warning of what might happen next, either to the market or a sub category, such as an industry group. One of the groups that typically provide a great leadership role, both on the upside and downside, are stockbrokers. This is because their profits are determined by the overall direction of the market. If prices are rising, there are more opportunities to bring profitable **IPO's**, or initial public offerings, to market. Rising prices mean that customers are more willing to actively trade, and that translates into more commissions. Market participants buy and sell any stock because of its profit potential or lack thereof. Therefore, it is natural that brokers should lead the market, just as the market leads the economy. Starting somewhere between the very late stage of a bear market and the start of a bull market, brokerage stocks have a strong tendency to outperform the overall market (Figure 14.1). Then, as the cycle matures and inflation takes hold, interest rates begin to rise and brokerage stocks tend to peak out, especially in a relative strength sense. During this period, their leadership role reverses to a downside role (Figure 14.2). Even during the early to middle phase of the cycle, when the overall trend of brokers is positive, it is not a one-way street. These stocks still experience moments of both absolute and relative weakness. The balance of this chapter focuses on this early to mid-phase of the cycle.

Using Brokers as Market Leaders

Chart 14.1 displays the Telescan Broker Index in the upper panel and the daily close for the S&P Composite in the middle. The relative strength of the brokers appears in the lower panel. A rising RS line means the brokers are outperforming the market, and a falling one means that they are not doing so well. All the

Figure 14.1 Primary Trend

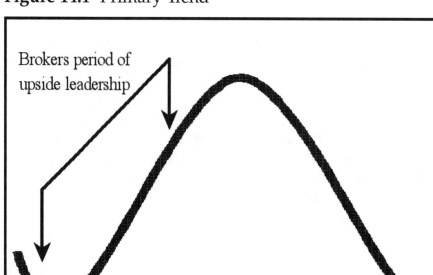

Figure 14.2 Primary Trend

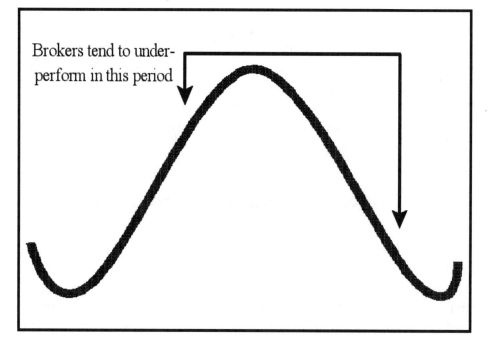

averages have a 30-day time period. Obviously, these are not intraday charts. I chose them because they do offer some perspective for intraday activity. In other words, when a relationship change is signaled on the daily chart, this new trend should immediately be translated into the shorter timeframes found on the intraday charts. These trend changes can be signaled with a moving average crossover, trendline break, or any other legitimate trend reversal technique.

Let us take a closer look at the brokers. During the September/November period, the brokers kept making new highs. This indicates investors were confident these companies were going to earn higher profits—in effect, anticipating a higher stock market. Every time the brokers bottomed and started to rally, so did the market. As long as this relationship held, it would have paid to trade brokerage stocks from the long side in the intraday charts. You can see that the relative strength line remained above its moving average during this whole period. Then, in mid-November (A), all three series broke below their averages and up trendlines. It was not until late December (B) that all series moved into positive territory again. Realistically, there are really two points to consider here: First, when all three series are in positive trends (indicated on the chart by being above their moving averages) higher prices should be expected. Second, if the Brokerage Index bottoms out, or breaks above a trendline along with its RS line, then expect the rest of the market, as reflected in the S&P, to move higher.

Looking again at Chart 14.1, you can see that all three series violated their moving averages in late January 1992. Even though the S&P was able to rally in April, there was really no response from the brokers, who continued to work their way lower. Chart 14.2 shows what happened next. The S&P went sideways and the brokers continued lower until June. Then, all three series violated down trendlines signaling a rally. In October, the Brokers rallied up to their major bear trendline, and the S&P moved back to its previous high. It had even attempted a prior breakout in September, but the brokers, who quickly moved below their moving average, did not confirm this. The really strong bull signal developed in October when the brokers and their RS broke above major down trendlines and their moving averages. This indicated that brokers once again had the upper hand and that we should

Chart 14.1   Telescan Brokers and Two Indicators

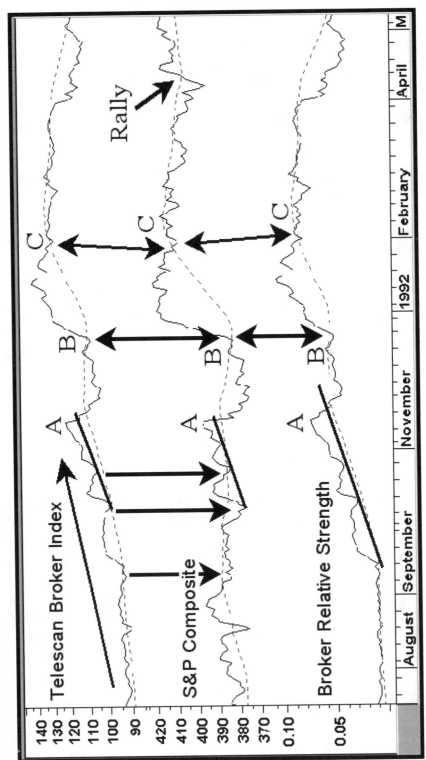

Chart 14.2   Telescan Brokers and Two Indicators

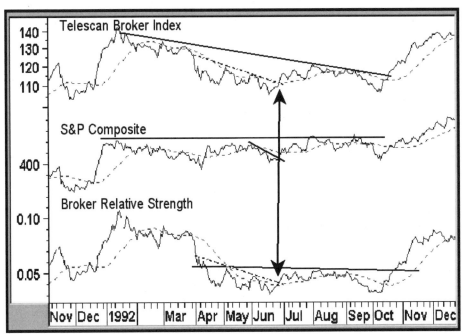

expect the market to follow. It did a few sessions later, by rallying above the resistance trendline. You can now see that in this stage of the bull market it is possible for the S&P to rally without the brokers, but the rally is usually very limited. It is only when all three series are in a rising trend that the S&P rally gets legs.

This analysis may appear to be taking us a long way from 5-minute bar charts and the like, but remember, it is important to have some perspective of the relationship between a leader and a laggard, because the leaders give warnings of what is likely to come and this can set the trading scene for the intraday charts.

Using Merrill Lynch as a Leader

This leadership function does not necessarily have to come from an industry group. It could be an actively traded stock. Chart 14.3 features Merrill Lynch against the S&P. I should add that during the period covered by the chart, Merrill had already been established as a market leader on the upside. You can see how MER was trading sideways through late Tuesday and Wednesday, whereas the S&P was moving lower. This relative outperformance by Merrill was an indication that the decline in the S&P may not run much further. The thing to look for was a breakout, either by MER, or both MER and the S&P. As it turned out, early on Thursday morning (A), both series broke convincingly to the upside indicating higher prices. Thursday afternoon price action is most revealing since it shows the market selling off late in the day. MER, however, holds its gains and refuses to follow suit or even lead the S&P lower. Note how both series rally and break out simultaneously by the Thursday close. At the opening bell on Friday, both series literally explode to the upside. Now, if we look at this situation with greater perspective (Chart 14.4), you can see the stock was breaking out from a 3-month consolidation pattern. This was not only a good omen for MER, but because of its leading tendencies, it was good for the market as a whole.

This is the type of analysis that could also be done with a leading technology stock and the NASDAQ or NASDAQ 100. By

Chart 14.3   Telescan Brokers vs. the S&P Composite

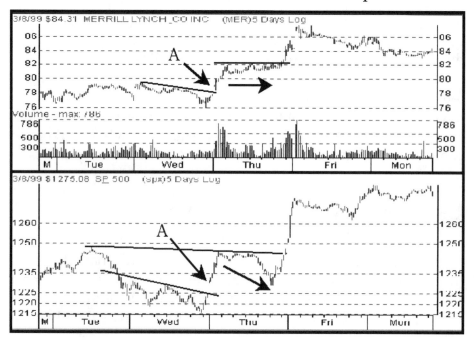

"leading" I mean a stock that is currently in fashion. It could be a key semiconductor stock, a computer manufacturer, an Internet stock, and so forth. The important thing is that market participants are focusing on a particular company and trade off its price action. Late in the cycle, when the Dow and commodity driven stocks are rallying, it would be possible to use a basic industry stock as a market leader, provided, of course, it had already demonstrated superior relative strength and so forth.

Trade Liquidity

Many people think that paying commissions is the major cost of trading. In the long run, though, the cost of consistently bad fills can be far more expensive. That is why it pays to concentrate your efforts in **liquid markets**, where spreads between bids and offers are relatively narrow and the cost of slippage is small. Chart

Chart 14.4   Telescan Brokers vs. the S&P Composite

14.5 features a 1-minute bar of March 1997 crude oil. As you can see, it is a pretty **illiquid market**. Look at the space between the 28th and the 29th. There should be literally hundreds of bars representing several hours of trading. There is clearly far less—indicating this contract was not traded that often during the day. At the time, this was a **delayed delivery**; i.e., a contract that was well away from the spot month. Nearby contracts are, of course, far more liquid. The reason I showed this particular example is to demonstrate two points. First, illiquid contracts do not lend themselves well to technical analysis. Second, it makes it very difficult to place stops and expect reasonable fills when a market is illiquid. The less liquid the market, the more you will be paying the floor in terms of slippage.

Compare the above situation to Chart 14.6 of December 1997 corn. This trading activity is not what I would call AAA quality, but at least there is sufficient volume to allow us to construct trendlines with the one-minute bars. This period encompassed regular price action. However, when unexpected news breaks, even what is normally a very liquid market can quickly experi-

Chart 14.5   March 1997 Crude Oil

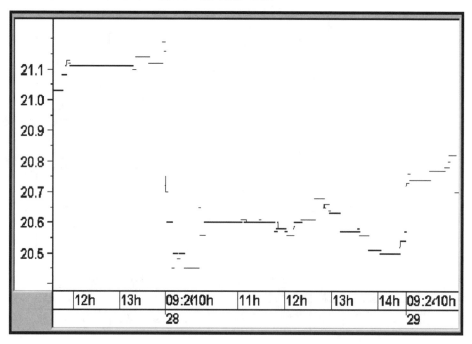

ence illiquid conditions for a minute or two, as everyone heads for the exits at the same time.

Illiquid markets can come from various sources. Perhaps it is a stock with a small float that does not trade very often. It could, as I mentioned earlier, develop from a deferred, or far out, futures contract where few people, apart from market makers, wish to participate. Finally, illiquidity can arise from a market that is traded in a time zone different from the principal location. Chart 14.7 represents a daily bar of the Nikkei traded in Tokyo. Not much problem with the right hand side of the chart as the contract approaches delivery, but you can see from the patchy action on the left-hand side, there are lots of gaps, meaning trading would have been very difficult. On the other hand, Chart 14.8 is slightly different because here, the Nikkei is being traded in the US. However, there can be no mistaking the huge number of gaps, even as the contract approached delivery. We can go so far as to say that the bars, which do not contain gaps, are the exception, and gaps are the rule. This is because the primary market for Japanese stocks is in Japan, not the US. All the US contract is really doing is trad-

Chart 14.6   December 1997 Corn 1-minute Bar

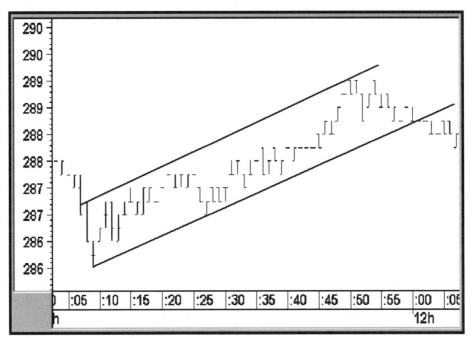

Chart 14.7   Japanese Nikkei Daily Bar

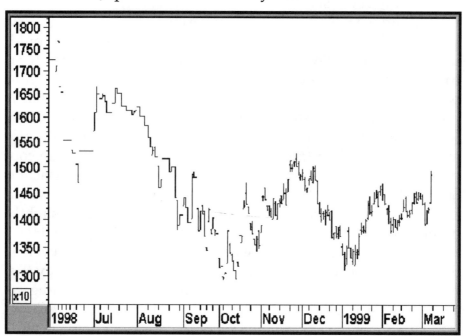

ing around the closes in Tokyo. Occasionally, there is a little price action during the US sessions, but not very much—hardly the kind of action desired by either short-term traders or day traders.

Treatment of News

A lot of people think news drives markets. This is incorrect because the markets discount, or anticipate, the news before it breaks. Occasionally, there are events that cannot be anticipated, but again, it is not the news that is important, but the market's *reaction* to the news.

If market participants are anticipating good earnings and those earnings come through, chances are the price will come down. This is because all those who were correctly anticipating the news will decide to take profits. If it comes in better than expected, and the price still declines, it indicates the technical situation is very weak. Ask yourself the question: If better than anticipated news

Chart 14.8   Japanese Nikkei Daily Bar (US)

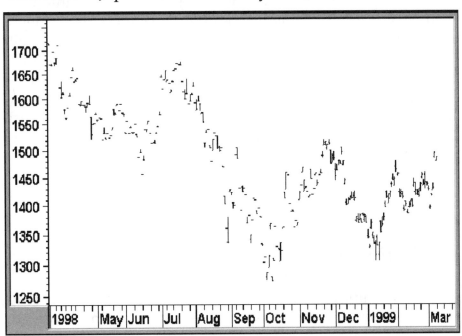

will not push prices higher, what will? The same principle would apply in reverse.

Take a look at the gold market in the 1980's when Anwar Sadat, president of Egypt, was assassinated. The gold price immediately rallied, but fell back below the existing price when the news broke. Gold prices are supposed to thrive on uncertainty and instability, so the failure of the price to hold its gains indicated a very weak market technically. In retrospect, it was a bear market.

In late 1979, the Russian invasion of Afghanistan resulted in a several hundred-dollar rise in the gold price. In this case, the instability was to be the *icing* on the gold bull market *cake* as we can see from Chart 14.9. On the other hand, the invasion of Kuwait in the summer of 1990 was responsible for a much smaller price move, yet, the inflationary implications due to uncertainties in the oil supply were much greater. The reason is that the Afghan invasion occurred in a bull market, and the Kuwait invasion developed in a bear market. The response to both would have been in keeping with what one would have expected on the intraday charts, since prices in each instance rallied sharply over the short-term.

This point demonstrates that if a market or stock's response to the news is not what is expected, you can, and should, use this information as an additional indicator in the "weight of the evidence approach." For example, if the news is good and the stock sells off, chances are the trendline break you were going to use as a shorting signal will be that much more reliable since the new trend is being supported by the market's perverse reaction to good news. In this case, we are using the behavioral aspects of market participants as a supplementary indicator to our regular technical analysis. By the same token, if you already have a long position, there is no sense in rushing to sell at $49 if a market responds adversely to bad news unless your pre-arranged stop point at $48 is hit.

Anticipate a Catalyst

We have already established it is not the news, but the reaction of the market to the news, which is important. In this respect,

Chart 14.9   Spot London Gold

it makes sense to anticipate a possible news-breaking story that could act as a catalyst and bring about important intraday price movements. Obvious events that come to mind are the release of specific economic numbers or testimony by the Federal Reserve Chairman to various congressional committees. Perhaps the most notorious market-moving statistic for both bonds and stocks is the Employment Report released on the first Friday of the month. Chart 14.10 shows the June 1999 bond contract. Notice how the price had been falling in anticipation of a report indicating a strong economy. However, when the report came out, the news was in line with expectations. Since the market had already factored this news into the price, a sharp rally began as soon as the report was released. The price closed half way up the trading range that day, and continued to work its way higher in the days that followed. This is a great example of why you should always be wary of buying into a report when the anticipated news is going with the previous trend. In other words, if the news is expected to be bad and prices decline, all the selling has probably been done. Short positions have been established, and weak owners have sold.

Chart 14.10 June 1999 Bonds Daily

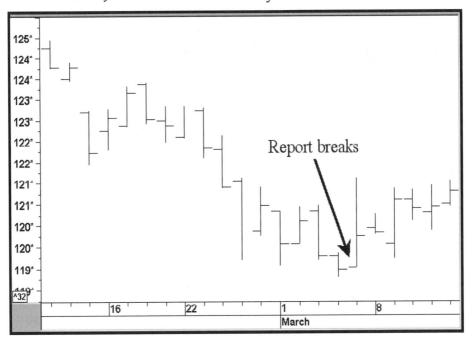

Unless the news is far, far worse than expected, the odds favor a rally on the report, or at worst, a quick 15-minute sell-off followed by a rally. The point to buy, in this case, would be when the price recovers to a higher level than when the report was released. After all, if the release of the report cannot keep the price down, what will?

The reverse is true in a rising market. If a stock rises in anticipation of a good earnings report for several days, it will be at its most vulnerable once the report is released. Many money managers delay selling until a good earnings report is released, or put off buying a stock until the expected bad news is out. For the day trader, this means waiting to see what the price will do once a good earnings report is released. If it declines when it should rally, its response is bearish, and the stock should be sold or shorted.

In the currency markets, trade statistics can occasionally act as market movers and so can so-called "G7 meetings," although these are not of much use to day traders since the meetings invariably take place over the weekend when the markets are closed.

Other catalysts include breaking news on leading stocks. For example, if Compaq releases a good earnings report that reflects rising sales and fat profit margins, it will not only act as a catalyst for Compaq, but other companies in the same business.

Using Intermarket Relationships as a Catalyst

Finally, you can look for catalysts in the form of intermarket relationships. Rising bond yields, for instance, usually translate into falling stock prices.

Chart 14.11 features the S&P Composite together with the 30-year yield. The yield series has been plotted inversely to correspond with bond prices. During July and August, both series move irregularly higher. In early August, bonds diverge negatively with stocks, and this was the first sign of trouble. However, the deterioration in bonds was not sufficient to act as a catalyst for stocks. Bonds then break a trendline (A) just after stocks peak out and, in retrospect, the strong upside equity momentum is broken. Bonds fall sharply after the trendline break, but stocks do not. Consequently, when the bond pressure is lifted at (B) with a small rally, stocks follow suit with a larger rally. Bonds immediately decline to a new low, which is a signal to anticipate equity weakness. This comes with a (B) trendline break, so stocks have now confirmed the bond break that took place earlier. Since bonds also violate a trendline (D) joining two lows, you know they are headed lower. Once again, we see a small rally in bonds at (E), which has a **multiplier effect** on stocks, completely out of proportion to that of bonds. However, stocks are unable to rally to new highs (F), which shows that deteriorating bond prices are having some overall effect. Now I want to show you a very subtle, but extremely important change in this relationship.

Look at Chart 14.12 where the strength of the bond rally can be more easily compared to the stock rally. The bond multiplier effect is still present at (A). Even when bonds start to head down, the S&P is still rallying. The bond advance at (B) also has a favorable effect. Compare rally (B) to the rally that begins at (C), a good bond rally, but virtually no response from stocks. Some-

Chart 14.11 S&P Composite vs. Government Bond Yield

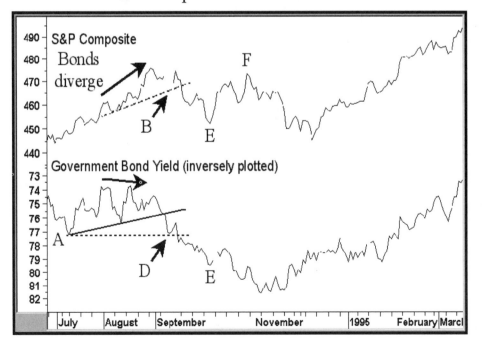

thing very different has started to happen. The strength in bonds is no longer having a multiplier effect on stocks. It is now a "reverse multiplier," if you will. This sets up a positive divergence at (C), where bonds rally and securities decline. Just as the negative divergence warned of trouble before, the positive divergence now places us on alert for a potential rally in equities. What is needed is for stocks to confirm with a signal. In Chart 14.13 we see this in the form of a rally above the trendline (E). Sure enough, both series rise in tandem again. Also, note how the quick setback in bonds at (F) no longer has a weakening effect on stocks. We are back to the positive multiplier effect again. At (G) we see bonds breaking slightly to the upside, and stocks at major resistance at trendline (A). Since we now know that bonds have probably begun a period when they have a multiplier effect on equities, the odds favor an upside breakout for the S&P. What is interesting is that as bonds falter a bit above the breakout level (H), stocks start to edge their way through resistance. This is a subtle, but extremely important point. We know that bonds have broken out from this small consolidation and are likely to rally. We can also see that

Chart 14.12 S&P Composite vs. Government Bond Yield

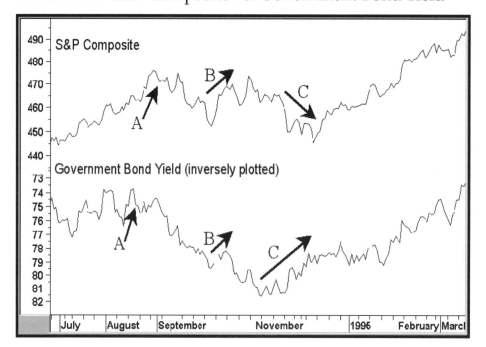

Chart 14.13 S&P Composite vs. Government Bond Yield

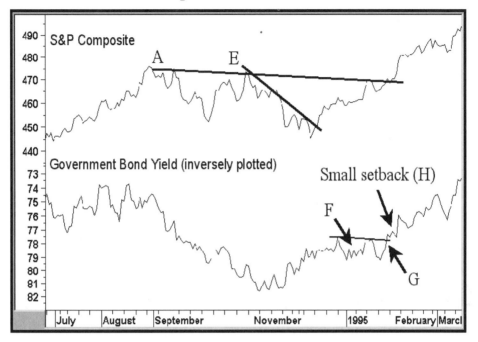

stocks are not responding to this small weakness in bonds. The $64,000 question then is: What will happen to stocks when the rally in bonds extends? The answer is that they virtually explode to the upside.

Summary of the Stock/Bond Relationship

1. Use daily charts to establish perspective concerning the responsiveness of stocks to bonds.

2. When stocks are responsive to bonds, on the upside we can use intraday charts to establish positive bond reversals to anticipate positive stock reversals.

3. When the relationship breaks down, bond weakness can be used to enable short sales in equities.

4. When the bond multiplier effect starts up again, following a sharp stock sell-off, the possibility of an explosive equity rally exists.

This example took place in a bull market environment, so the opposite will occur in a bear market where declining bonds will have the multiplier effect again, but this time on the downside. (Other sectors, which the equity market occasionally uses to trade off, include the dollar, commodity, and to a lesser extent, gold prices.) In order to use any of these markets for the purposes of day trading the S&P or individual stocks, it is first necessary to establish that a close relationship is currently in force. This can either be done by studying the charts themselves, or by monitoring observations made by journalists and other commentators and relating them to market response or, in fact, both.

Think in Terms of Probabilities

In technical analysis, all we are really doing is dealing in probabilities—the probability that the trend has reversed. Thus, as traders, it is important for us to think in terms of probabilities, while simultaneously measuring the risks of our trades. It is impossible to place precise odds on any trade. However, the more pieces of evidence that indicate a trend has reversed, the greater the probability it has. Take Chart 14.14, for example. Here we see a nice double breakout to the upside. Looks good, doesn't it? However, this snapshot only looks at one piece of evidence that a rally is likely to take place. We can also see that it eventually failed. Obviously, we need more evidence than the price action to increase the probabilities that the trade will be successful. Chart 14.15 shows the same situation, but this time I have introduced several indicators. The first is a 14-period RSI. You can see how it completed and broke down from a top earlier in the day at (A). This is a negative piece of evidence. Even at the time of the breakout, the RSI was overbought. Worse still, is the position of the long-term 15-minute KST. This series was actually in the process of peaking as the breakout was taking place. Summing it all up, the breakout was a positive sign, but RSI momentum was not encouraging, nor was the longer-term perspective as painted by the

Chart 14.14 December 1997 Corn 15-minute Bar

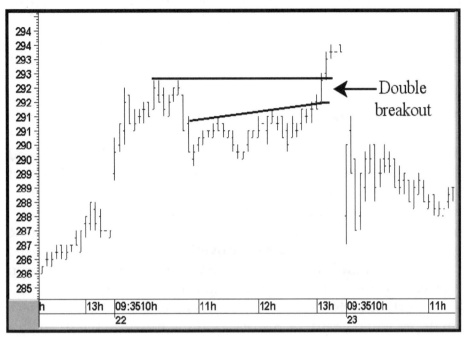

Chart 14.15 December 1997 Corn 15-minute Bar

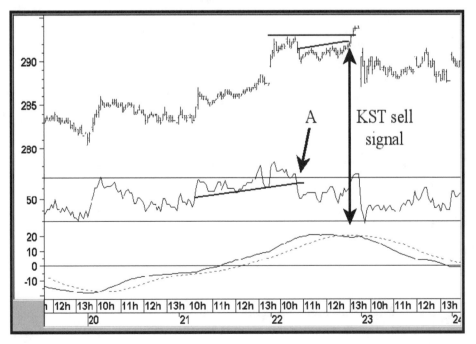

KST. In fact, this indicator was downright bearish. The probability that the trade would be profitable was not zero, but clearly very low.

Now, let us take a look at the breakout of a 15-minute bar chart of the NYSE Composite in Chart 14.16. We see the price test its low at (A), and then rallies to a new recovery high (B). This set in motion a series of rising peaks and troughs. What are the probabilities of this one working out? Well, there is another piece of bullish evidence we can point to and that is a breakout from the down trendline (C), and a breakout from an upward sloping head and shoulders pattern. The neckline is flagged by the upward sloping dashed trendline.

Now, if we look at Chart 14.17, we can see the RSI had previously broken above a down trendline (A). By the time of the breakout, the RSI was moderately overbought, which reduced the probabilities of a breakout somewhat. However, the long-term KST was oversold and had begun to turn up (B). This suggested an important bottom had been seen. As it turned out, there was a small price to be paid for the overbought RSI since the price, im-

Chart 14.16 NYSE Composite 15-minute Bar

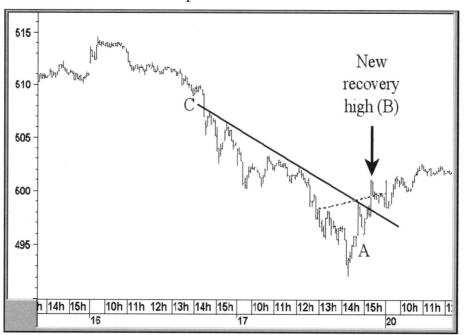

Chart 14.17 NYSE Composite 15-minute Bar

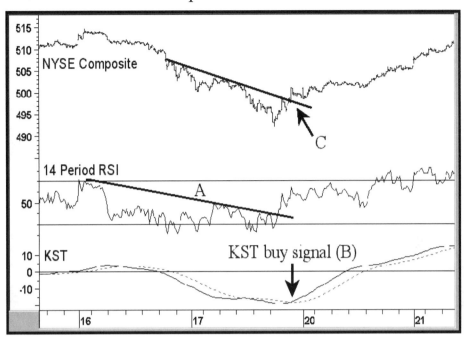

mediately following the breakout, fell back to the level of the previous high (C). After that, there was no looking back.

Chart 14.18 shows another interesting period. The bear trend was punctuated with declining peaks and troughs until (A), when the price broke above the previous high. This was preceded by an upside break of trendline (C), which indicated that downside momentum had dissipated. We can also see that the RSI broke above a trendline (E), so the probabilities of a profitable trade had increased. However, the long-term KST was still in a declining phase and told us that, while the decline was mature, it could go further. This should have made us suspicious about the breakout, unless we were of the belief that the price and RSI action were sufficiently bullish to reverse the downward trajectory of the KST. What happened, was the day of the breakout proved to be the high for the move. After this, the price slowly, but surely, eroded. Liquidation, especially with the benefit of hindsight, could have taken place with a break below the minor low by the arrow at (B) in Chart 14.18. A last ditch stop would have been placed below the trendline joining the three previous lows, at (D). Altogether,

Chart 14.18 NYSE Composite 15-minute Bar

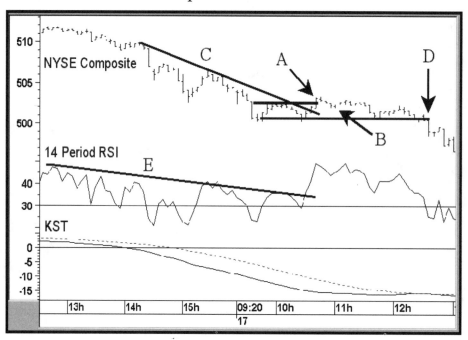

Chart 14.19 NYSE Composite 15-minute Bar

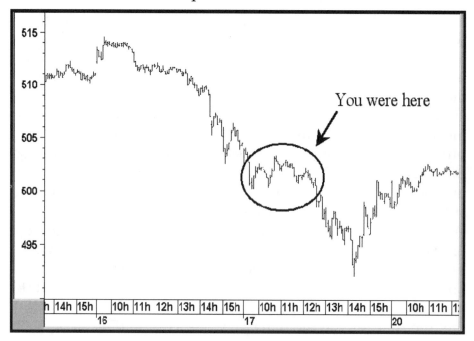

this situation was a bit iffy from the beginning, because of the downward moving KST. Had we decided to take the plunge, it would have been wiser to tighten the stop as closely as possible, in view of the potential treachery of the situation.

The circle in Chart 14.19 shows the false breakout that developed in Chart 14.18 was just over halfway down the decline. This whipsaw also demonstrates that if something is going to go wrong, it will usually happen when the signal develops in the opposite direction of the prevailing trend. ■

Chapter 15 ——————————————————

Ten Tips to Control
Your Emotions

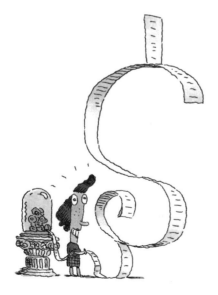

The following tips, if understood and applied, will help you become a successful day trade warrior.

1. Don't Trade at the Edge of the Pendulum Swing

Essentially, it is changes in group psychology that drive prices as they alternate from the extremes of greed to panic and fear. Obviously, you do not wish to be part of the crowd by buying at the high and selling at the low. Unfortunately, the crowd is made up of individuals who are subject to the same emotions that affect you. The ultimate key to successful trading—more important than any technique, piece of knowledge, or years of experience—is being able to *master your own emotions*. If you can learn to avoid becoming euphoric when things go well, or depressed when adversity strikes, you have accomplished the single most important step on the way to successful trading.

2. Pring's Law

Anything that stimulates your emotions will also increase your odds of making a mistake. *Pring's law states that, other things being equal, trading success is inversely related to emotional stimulation.* The more excited you get, the less likely you are to make money. The "other things being equal" was included to account for the fact that some people get downright lucky some of the time. Just as people become fortunate in casinos, traders can get lucky in the markets. Over time, though, Pring's law will, unfortunately, win out. For example, suppose you have just taken a position in the S&P Futures and you have a good profit from the breakout at (A) in Chart 15.1. You then see the possibility of another breakout (B). You can, again, add to your position at (C), and again at (D). Every time you do, more and more profits are earned. Finally, confidence and greed overpower you, and at (E) another breakout develops. Perhaps doubling the position and taking a few points will help you get that luxury car you have always wanted.

Chart 15.1   S&P Composite 30-minute Bar

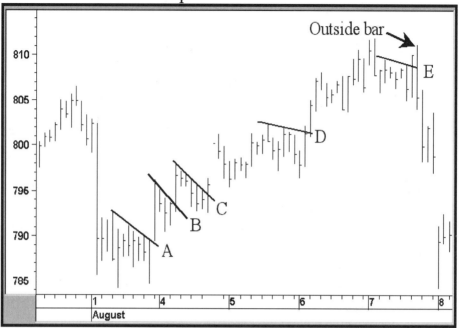

So, you go for it. Now look what happened. Instead of repeating the rallies of the past, the market experiences an outside bar and starts to come down with a vengeance.   Instead of making more money, your overconfidence got you into trouble right at the top. Chart 15.2 offers one reason why the last breakout was unsuccessful. The smoothed momentum in the lower panel, which had been on your side during the rally, has begun to roll over in an ominously bearish manner. Overconfidence not only leads to mistakes of this kind, but can also encourage you to take positions in other markets, or stocks, where the technical conditions do not favor profits—your wishes for gain are fathering your thought processes. This exuberance also discourages a quiet approach to stalking your trades and doing research. Since you have made money in one market, you throw your usual caution to the wind, and try to duplicate this success elsewhere.

Chart 15.2 S&P Composite 30-minute Bar

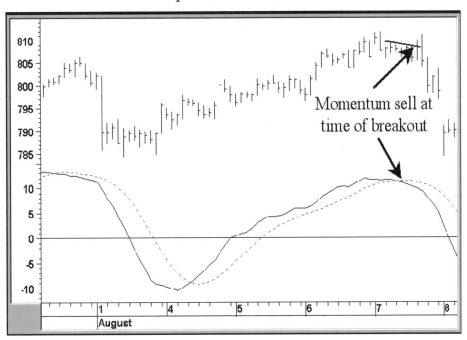

3. Only Trade with a Balanced Mindset

Success, if you let it, breeds carelessness. This leads to badly thought-out trading and eventually to serious losses. As a result, your emotions swing in the opposite direction and lead you to despondency and despair. In this type of situation, you lose confidence and are quickly stopped out of positions where you would normally be more careful. Whenever you feel yourself being pulled by either of these emotions, the best thing to do is stop trading. After all, if you liked playing tennis and were good at it, would you really consider playing if you had a serious bout of the flu? Of course not, because you would know that you could not possibly play a good game while under the weather. It could be seriously detrimental to your overall health. The same is true in trading. You must be in a good, balanced state of mind or else you will run into serious losses. It is easy to ignore obvious trading opportunities when you are not in the right state of mind. I can give you a personal experience to let you know that even the best traders make mistakes. It is shown in Chart 15.3. Although it is not an intraday example, the principle is identical. In the spring of 1997, I shorted the market by buying the Rydex Ursula Fund (A). You make money when **shorting** if the market declines, and lose money when it rallies. The decision to go short was based on the fact the S&P had completed and broken down from a head and shoulders pattern—a perfectly logical and legitimate decision. The position worked for a while, as you can see. Then, the market turned around and the S&P broke out from a reverse head and shoulders pattern (B). I knew this to be a bull market, so I covered my position. As it turned out, that was the right thing to do. However, the market broke out from the pattern with incredible violence. I knew that it was headed much higher, but I could not bring myself to go long because I just lost money on the long side. It was a bull market and a new up leg was beginning. I was convinced of that, yet, I was not of the right state of mind to take any action. The other mistake was shorting in the first place, since this was a contra-trend trade, and I had absolutely no evidence, at the time, that the longer-term trend had signaled a bear market.

Chart 15.3   S&P Composite Daily Bar

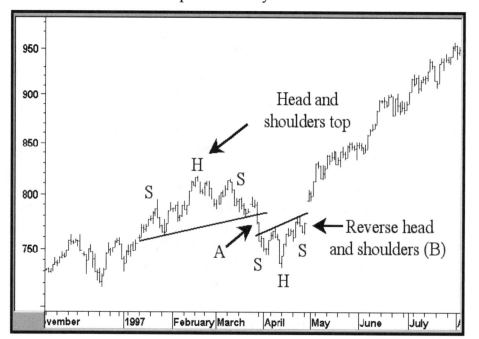

4. Patience and Discipline—Required Ingredients for Successful Trading

Having the right state of mind also involves patience, as well as discipline. Chart 15.4 shows a breakout from a reverse head and shoulders pattern (A). It is possible you may have missed the breakout, but patience would have given you a second chance as the price fell back to the breakout level fairly soon. You would not have wanted it at this point, since the whole up move was in question. Even if you had bought on the breakout, it would have been necessary to adopt a flexible stance. The price objective called for a rally to (X), which could well have been the place where you planned to sell. As you can see, it never made it. The flexibility involved taking a bearish stance once the small head and shoulders was completed (B). This pattern was much smaller than the inverse formation, so it would have been reasonable to expect a pull back to the top of the large formation as a normal retracement move. However, once a pattern like this has been completed, it is often a good idea to protect profits and run scared, because you never know. In this instance, the price fell almost to the level of the head, in the inverse head and shoulders pattern (C). Also, notice how bottoms and tops often cancel each other out. We saw one example of a small head and shoulders canceling a larger inverse head and shoulders. Now look at the inverse head and shoulders formed between the 18th and 23rd (D). See how a small triple top temporarily canceled it out when it was completed at (E). The ensuing decline was not as serious as the decline from the previous head and shoulders top, but since a trend is only as good as the last signal, it would certainly have paid to liquidate on the completion of the triple top. Sometimes, though, patience does not pay. If you missed the breakout in Chart 15.5 you never got another chance to get in. That is why, if you are trading, make sure you give it 100% of your attention.

Chart 15.4   S&P Composite 30-minute Bar

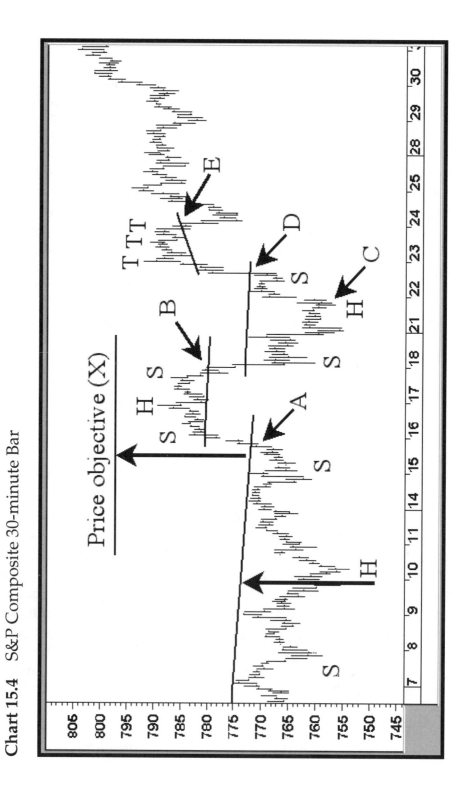

Chart 15.5 S&P Composite 30-minute Bar

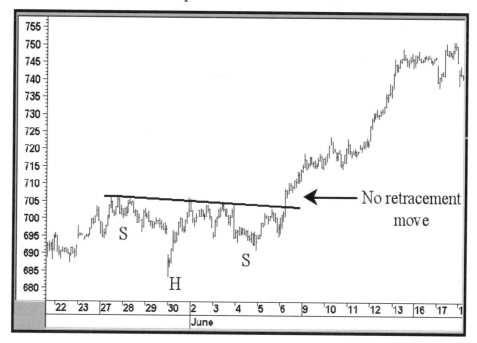

5. Only Trade When You Feel Good and There is an Obvious Opportunity; Do Not Trade Merely Because You Want To

You can spend all the time in the world reading books and studying techniques, but it will not help if you are in the wrong state of mind. As I mentioned before, one of the absolute keys to successful trading is to keep your emotions as subdued as possible. If you enter a position when you do not feel good about trading, then you are guaranteed to lose money when things start to go against you. For example, if you have absolute confidence (as opposed to overconfidence) in what you are doing, adverse price movements will only cause ripples in your emotions. While there may be a few hitches in your game plan, it is still possible to steer a straight course ahead. If you do not feel good about your trading, the slightest adverse condition will raise doubts about your strategies and tactics. This, in turn, can result in a bad decision, such as getting out of a position prematurely, etc.

Take a look at Chart 15.6. As it opens, the price of the NYSE December 1997 contract is declining. Then, let us say you recognize the market is destined to move higher because the price breaks above the neckline of a reverse head and shoulders pattern. At the time of the breakout (A), you are out of the room looking for a cup of coffee. Because you did not put a stop into the market, the price rocketed away and you missed your opportunity. Feeling angry with yourself, you turn off the screen and do something else. Then a little later, you still feel a bit curious and turn the computer on again and see that this one-minute bar chart has now indicated that the price not only fell back to the extended neckline, but has also rallied. Now, you are really angry because you could have placed an order at the trendline and the price is getting away again. To eradicate your frustration, you buy into the rally at (B). Since the 14:48 low looks like a good one, you construct a trendline (X) joining the low for the move to the 14:48 low. You are now on board, but at 15:10 (C), some news comes out that sends the price down slightly. A small top has now been completed (D), and your unbalanced emotions tell you to liquidate since you "know" this news will send the price much lower. After all, the price failed to rally above the previous high, so the resistance must be considerable. Remember, the game plan is to stop yourself out when the up trendline is violated. At this point, it had not happened, but in your own mind the weak price action is telling you that it is certain to do so. This is often one of the most difficult things to do—stick to the game plan when the market is going against you. If there is a good technical reason to get out, then do so, but do not project where the market will go based on news. In this case, the small double top was really inconsequential, but its completion was magnified by your interpretation of the news, *a deadly combination.* Remember that you came into the trade in a state of frustration and a feeling of just having to get on board. Emotions swing like a pendulum and in this case the news and small breakdown caused the pendulum to swing from greed to fear. After a few bars, the market shrugs off the news and rallies sharply. In retrospect, the decline that got you out was very small, but at the time it seemed to be big. Had you been in the right state of mind, you would not have tricked yourself out of the position. But, because you lacked the confidence to stay the

Chart 15.6   NYSE Composite 1-minute Bar

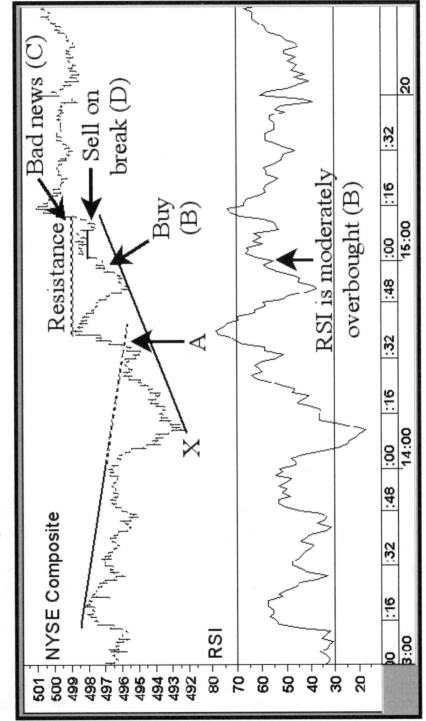

course and keep to the game plan, you were shaken out too early. In this instance, the trade ended in a small profit, but this was just the luck of the draw. It could easily have turned into something far worse. Now, if you study the lower section of Chart 15.6, you can see the RSI was moderately overbought at the time of the purchase. I mention this because however much you might want to buy or sell, if you see an oscillator in an extreme, or even moderately extreme position, do not act on it. That is—unless the extreme is an oversold in the case of a buy, or an overbought for a short sale. I am not going to say that overboughts and oversolds never work, because sometimes they do. The odds usually are not in your favor, though, and remember it is the odds and probabilities with which we are concerned.

6. If You Get in for a Good Reason, Get Out if it No Longer Remains Valid

When most of us make a trading decision, we have a high degree of confidence it is going to work out. The trade is entered on the basis of certain factors, breakouts buying into support, selling into resistance, and so forth. In our enthusiasm, or more likely dogmatism, we, unfortunately, pay little or no attention when the conditions that originally put us into the trade no longer apply. It is so easy to turn a blind eye or rationalize why the trade will work in our favor. It is called "**pride of opinion**." Charles Dow, the founder of technical analysis, believed that pride of opinion was the greatest cause of financial ruin in the marketplace.

Chart 15.7 reflects a 5-minute bar chart of the NYSE Composite. See how a perfectly legitimate breakout took place after a decline (A). The reason to enter the trade was the breakout, pure and simple. Before we enter the order to buy, we must make an even more important decision. Where are we going to get out if things go against us? In this case, there are three possibilities: 1) below the low of the trading range (B), 2) below the low of the bar prior to the breakout (C), and 3) slightly below the breakout point marked by the trendline (D). My preference is below the trendline at (D), because that means if the price violates the trendline, the breakout is no longer in force. In many instances,

Chart 15.7   NYSE Composite 5-minute Bar

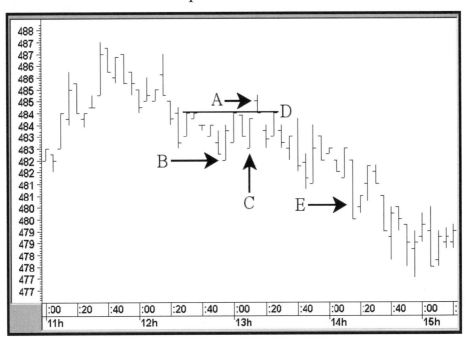

we find the price will stabilize and move back above the line, but at this point we just do not know.   From a trading aspect, what got us into the position is no longer valid because the price is below the breakout point. It just so happened that liquidating when the price broke below the trendline was a wise decision, since the price never broke back above it again. It, ever so gently, rallied and reacted, never really breaking down, that is until (E), after which, the erosion was quite severe.

The advantage of deciding when to admit defeat ahead of time prepared us mentally for taking a small loss—a small loss that could easily have turned into a large one.

Chart 15.8 shows a 5-minute bar chart of corn. You can see that the 14-bar RSI crossed below its overbought zone and violated an up trendline (A), which signaled that the trend of momentum had reversed to the downside. This was later confirmed with a break below support by the price itself. This confirmation would have represented a legitimate signal to go short. However, a couple of bars later, the price broke a little above the breakdown level. This did not invalidate the breakdown, but

Chart 15.8   December 1997 Corn 5-minute Bar

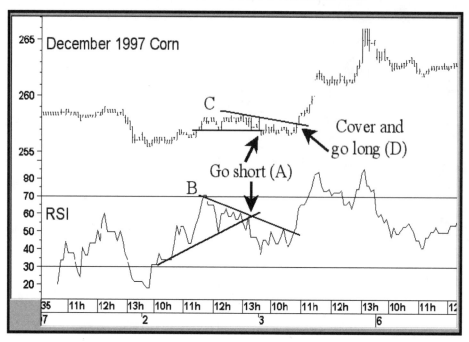

did increase the odds that it would fail. A really skeptical trader would now liquidate, since the object of the game is to preserve capital—only letting profits run when the odds are strongly in your favor. Let us say we stayed with the position, because the price immediately slips below the up trendline again. Actually, a trading range develops above and below the breakdown point. That, in and of itself, should provide us with a warning that the technical picture is not what we expected. After all, we can always go short again if the price breaks below this range, that is, provided the RSI is in a moderate overbought condition. Finally, the RSI broke above trendline (B), and this was later confirmed by the price (C). The conditions that encouraged us to put on the trade have clearly reversed. This fact should be admitted and the position should be liquidated, if we have not done so already. Now there are far more reasons to go long, actually reversing the position. As you can see, this was followed by a very worthwhile rally.

Chart 15.9 shows what happened later. The RSI breaks below the overbought zone (D). Those who trade solely on momentum would use this as an opportunity to go short. However, I prefer to wait for a price confirmation, which in this case, would be a break below the lower part of the (XY) trading range. Since the breakdown point is very close to the current price, very little in the way of profit would be given up. Let us suppose, though, a short position was entered in the belief that the price would decline. Before we can enter the trade, an important and essential decision must be made: Where do we get out if, on that outside chance, we are wrong? Once again, we are rehearsing the possibility that the anticipated scenario will not work. In going through this process, we are greatly reducing the potential for allowing pride of opinion to get in the way of a sound trading decision. In this case, the obvious place is just above resistance, as marked by the trendline (X). It would really have paid off because the price literally exploded to the upside. Our RSI, which did look as if it had peaked, then ran up above the overbought level again.

On the other hand, you may have noticed the momentum indicators were not in an oversold condition at the time of this breakout. This may have held you back. But that is fine because

Chart 15.9   December 1997 Corn 5-minute Bar

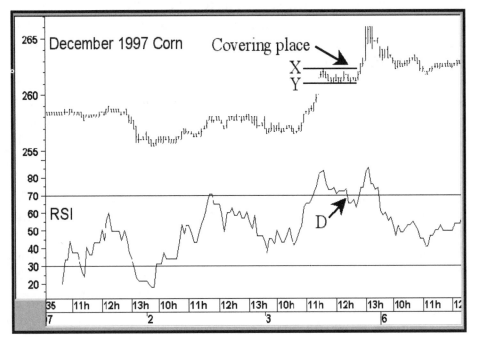

you want to make sure as many indicators as possible are pointing in the direction of the trade. That will give you the confidence to hold on to the position and not get prematurely shaken out. Remember, and this is extremely important, do not let yourself swing to a psychological pendulum extreme because you missed out on an opportunity. There is always another train leaving. You may think that one had your name engraved on it, but believe me, it is not worth getting worked up over it. Another opportunity is always around the corner.

7. Do Not Penny Pinch

One of the characteristics of *successful traders* is that he or she is imperfect and knows it. A characteristic of a *neophyte* is someone who continually strives for perfection. Perfection in markets is either impossible or extremely lucky—neither is the norm. In this case, when I talk about perfection, I am referring to the objective of buying at the absolute low and selling at the absolute high. We have already learned that the most successful traders lose more trades than they win. It is just that the wins are very profitable, and the losses are cut quickly. They know their first objective is not to lose money, and the second is to take home a profit. Notice I said profit, not a large profit, not a killing, but merely a profit. Small profits harvested over a long period will almost always win out over huge, but inconsistent profits.

Chart 15.10 shows a breakout from a consolidation. The upside objective is indicated by the upper horizontal line (A), which is a good place to sell. The price makes a good faith effort, but does not quite make it (B). Then, we see an outside bar (C), which closes near the top of the previous bar's range. There are now two reasons why it makes sense to take profits. First, the outside bar throws some doubt on the possibility of reaching the price pattern objective. Second, the opening range of the bar following the outside bar is so close to the objective that penny pinching for those last couple of dollars makes no sense at all. The name of the game is to make money, not to maximize profits on every trade. In this case, it would have made sense to take those profits because a nasty set back followed.

Chart 15.10 December 1997 Corn 5-minute Bar

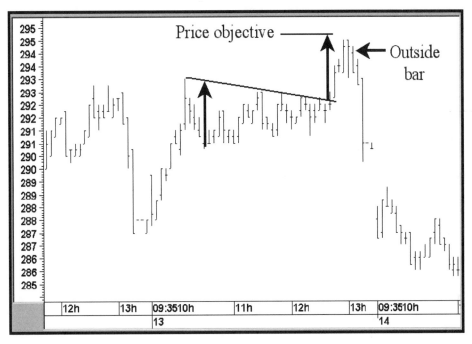

Chart 15.11 features a 9-period RSI. I am assuming the predominant trend is up, so I am stalking the corn price to see if I can buy it on the trendline. If it touches the line, I can place a close stop and can find out quickly whether I am right or wrong. I cannot afford to give it too much room by buying at the current price because the price action looks a bit like a head and shoulders top. At (A), the price is pretty close to the line, but not quite there. However, you can see that the RSI is now oversold. If my assumption about a bull trend is correct, the price may not go much lower because momentum indicators are very sensitive to oversold conditions in a bull market. Therefore, it makes sense to buy very close to the line and not penny pinch by trying to buy at a price that may never be seen. Consequently, I place my buy stop just a bit above the line (A), or even at a specified price, as the price closes in on the line. After all, the difference between the price during this last bar of trading and the line is very small. As you can see, the price never came down sufficiently to actually touch the line.

Chart 15.11 December 1997 Corn 5-minute Bar

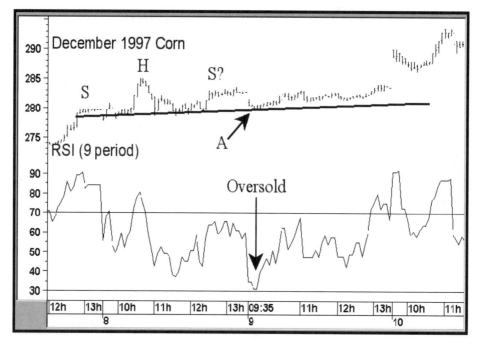

Of course, it does not work out this way every time. The point I am trying to make is that it does not make much sense to nickel and dime buying and selling decisions, because you stand the chance of missing out on worthwhile moves. The same would be true in a fast moving market. If you are convinced, based on the technical evidence, that a price is going to move much higher or lower, make sure you give your order enough room; otherwise, the market may get away from you. This is not the same thing as saying buy at any cost or liquidate at whatever price it takes. I am really referring to situations where you have carefully, methodically, and objectively thought out your tactics and strategy. If you have placed an order at a specific price and things are now moving away from you, take bolder action to ensure an execution, that is, provided you still have a good risk/reward ratio, and the price has not moved too far away from your stop loss point.

8. Trade Smaller Positions When Things Go Wrong

One of the most important principles of trading is cut losses short and let profits run. When things go wrong it could be pure bad luck, or the fact that your assumptions about some of the underlying trends are incorrect. If you have been taking a series of losses, it will also affect your confidence. Either way, it makes sense to trade smaller positions, so you can stem any further losses until you feel you have a better grip on the situation. As discussed earlier, if you do not feel good about yourself and do not have your normal degree of confidence, the slightest adversity will cause you to back out of what might otherwise be a perfectly good position.

Remember traders, just like sports people, have periods when they are off form. When you are playing a sport professionally, it is not a great idea, for financial reasons, to take time off when you are off form. The manager will do that for you sooner or later. However, it's fairly easy to tell when your trading form is off—you consistently lose money. Better to stop altogether, or grossly reduce those positions until things improve. I know several trading houses that recognize that traders have hot and cold spells. They tell them to suspend the account when losses reach certain targets. By the same token they actually take money away from traders if they make what they regard as too much money over too short a period. Such results, they argue, are too good to last. Either way, they are managing the expected ups and downs of their traders.

9. Not Sure? Don't Trade

Most of us sit in front of the computer screen with a strong desire to start trading. This does not mean that we should do so right away. It is important to make sure that the opportunity offers high probability to profit. If you are not sure, then do not trade. Chart 15.12 features a 5-minute corn chart again. Look at the resistance line (A). Would it not make sense to buy on a break

Chart 15.12 December 1997 Corn 5-minute Bar

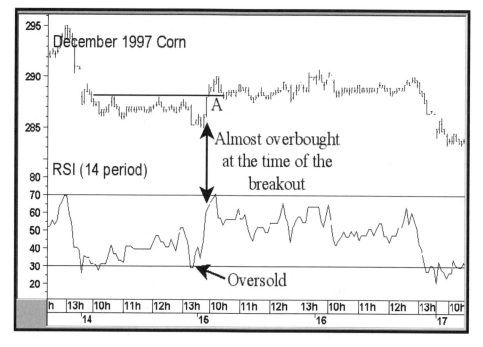

above it? Yes, I think it would make sense. After all, the 14-bar RSI is oversold. However, by the time the breakout has taken place, the RSI is close to an overbought condition. The thinking trader will no longer be as sure, since it will not take very much in terms of upward price movement before the RSI crosses above its overbought zone. As it turned out, that was pretty much all the move since the price moved sideways for a fairly long time prior to selling off. There are two reasons why a "not being sure" type of attitude is bad for making a trading decision. The first reason, as we have seen, is that you may have been misled due to conflicting technical evidence. The second has to do with confidence. As I discussed earlier, your state of mind is of paramount importance when entering a trade. If you are unsure going into a trade, the smallest adversity is likely to trip you out of the position, regardless of whether it is valid or not.

10. Take Time to Learn

A lot of people buy a computer, subscribe to a quote or charting service and begin to day trade. They do not pay attention to the fact that they really do not know very much about the business, and are risking their money against top rated professionals with a wealth of resources, experience and knowledge. In any other venture in life, rational people would take the trouble to learn the game—day trading is no different. If you are prepared to take lessons to learn to play a musical instrument or the game of golf, you should certainly take the time to study day trading. After your golf lessons, you will play against players close to your own ability or a little better. You would never think of playing and trying to beat a professional. Why should you expect to win at day trading against the pros? The only way you can compete is to have taken the trouble to learn. Trade slowly at first, gradually building up confidence and experience. Buying and watching this tutorial is a good first step. Now you need to put the theory slowly, but surely, into practice. Remember this thought when you are tempted to take those big risks. The vast majority of traders quit as losers in their first year. Make sure you are not one of them. ■

APPENDIX

Quiz

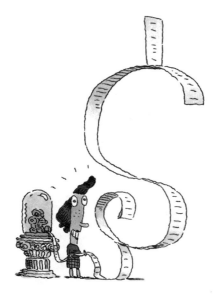

Question 1

What is the major difference between intraday and monthly bar charts?

☐ A. None whatsoever.

☐ B. Intraday charts are far more difficult to read.

☐ C. Time frames.

☐ D. Monthly charts are more difficult to read.

Question 2

What do gaps on intraday charts tell us?

☐ A. Traders have become highly emotional.

☐ B. The price will retrace the gap move because they are always filled.

☐ C. The data plot is incorrect.

☐ D. None of the above.

Question 3

Buy stops that liquidate a position should always be placed at support.

☐ A. True

☐ B. False

Question 4

Measuring objectives for price patterns are generally:

☐ A. Impossible to determine.

☐ B. Based on a different method depending on the type of price pattern.

☐ C. None of these answers.

☐ D. Based on the distance between the high and low of the pattern projected at the time of the breakout in its direction.

Question 5

What pointers indicate the probable direction of the stock market?

- ❑ A. The trend of interest rates.
- ❑ B. Market leaders such as brokerage stocks.
- ❑ C. A and B.
- ❑ D. The price of cocoa.

Question 6

The following are common mistakes made by traders:

- ❑ A. They try to be perfect instead of trying for excellence.
- ❑ B. They become too emotional.
- ❑ C. They think trading is just like any other business.
- ❑ D. All of the above.

Question 7

The best way to trade a market is:

- ❑ A. Go for broke.
- ❑ B. Consistently earn small profits.
- ❑ C. Cut losses quickly.
- ❑ D. Both B and C.

Question 8

Support and Resistance are:

- ❑ A. Points on a chart where the probabilities favor a temporary halt in the prevailing trend.
- ❑ B. Not as important as you may think.
- ❑ C. Selling and buying points.
- ❑ D. None of the above.

Question 9

If a resistance level is violated, you should:

- ❑ A. Go long.
- ❑ B. Go short.
- ❑ C. Cover a short position.
- ❑ D. Both A and C.

Question 10

If a support level is violated, the price:

- ❑ A. Is likely to rally.
- ❑ B. Is likely to go sideways.
- ❑ C. Both A and B.
- ❑ D. Fall to the next support level.

Question 11

Whenever you enter a trade, you should:

- ❑ A. Estimate the potential profit.
- ❑ B. Place a stop close to the entry price.
- ❑ C. Ask the question "What is my potential reward and what is my potential risk?"
- ❑ D. Both B and C.

Question 12

Gaps are:

- ☐ A. Important support/resistance areas.
- ☐ B. A reflection of strong emotions.
- ☐ C. Always filled.
- ☐ D. Both A and B.

Question 13

If a reaction retraces 5% of the previous rally this is normally regarded as a legitimate trough in peak and trough analysis.

- ☐ A. True.
- ☐ B. False.

Question 14

Could this bear market rally be regarded as a legitimate peak under peak and trough analysis?

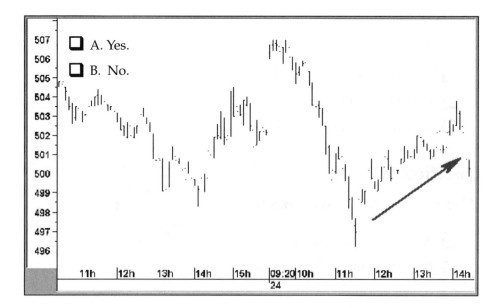

Question 15

Moving averages:

      ☐ A. Are almost pefect indicators.

      ☐ B. Rarely work on intraday charts.

      ☐ C. Are a useful indicator that should be used in conjunction with other indicators.

      ☐ D. Should always be used on their own without regard to other indicators.

Question 16

Which moving average crossover is likely to result in the more reliable buy signal?

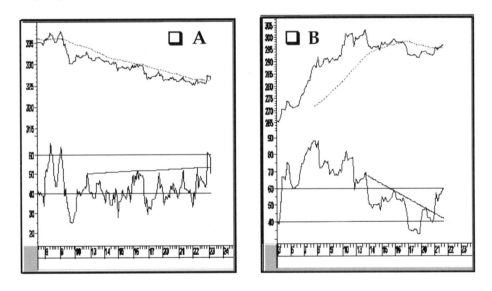

Question 17

Which of the following statements is correct?

      A. Momentum measures the velocity of a price move.

      B. The principles of momentum interpretation apply to all oscillators in one way or another.

      C. Momentum is a generic term embracing all oscillators.

      D. All of the above.

Question 18

A positive divergence is:

- ☐ A. Always followed by a rally.
- ☐ B. A sign of technical strength.
- ☐ C. Usually followed by another decline.
- ☐ D. A more powerful signal than a moving average crossover.

Question 19

Other things being equal, which signal should be followed by the strongest move?

- ☐ A. A trendline break of a 7-period ROC of a 30-minute bar.
- ☐ B. A trendline break of a 5-period ROC of a 60-minute bar.
- ☐ C. A trendline break of a 180-period ROC of a 10-minute bar.
- ☐ D. A trendline break of a 400-period of a 1-minute bar.

Question 20

Which of the following statements are true?

- ☐ A. A trendline break of a momentum indicator is a signal to buy or sell.
- ☐ B. A trendline break of a momentum indicator, when confirmed by a reversal signal in the price, is a signal to buy or sell.
- ☐ C. An overbought/oversold crossover is a stronger signal than a momentum trendline break.
- ☐ D. None of the above.

Question 21

Which, if any, of the following makes sense?

☐ A. Buy on a strong price trendline break when the oscillator is overbought.

☐ B. Sell on a strong up trendline break when the oscillator is over bought.

☐ C. Buy on a strong down trendline break when the oscillator is oversold.

☐ D. None of the above.

Question 22

The KST is almost a perfect indicator.

☐ A. True.

☐ B. False.

Question 23

It's not usually a good idea to go short when you expect a decline in a bull market.

☐ A. True.

☐ B. False.

Question 24

The KST is a useful indicator because it:

☐ A. Combines several ROC's of different time cycles into one indicator.

☐ B. Can be adapted to different time frames.

☐ C. Always changes direction at the same time as the price.

☐ D. Both A and B.

Question 25

Bollinger bands expand and contract depending on:

- ☐ A. The level of volatility.
- ☐ B. The direction of the price movement.
- ☐ C. The calculation of the simple moving average.
- ☐ D. None of the above.

Question 26

Looking at this chart and working on the probabilities, what is likely to happen next?

- ☐ A. The price rallies sharply.
- ☐ B. The price will decline.
- ☐ C. An important move will get underway as soon as the bands start to expand.
- ☐ D. The price will first break to the upside, and then to the downside.

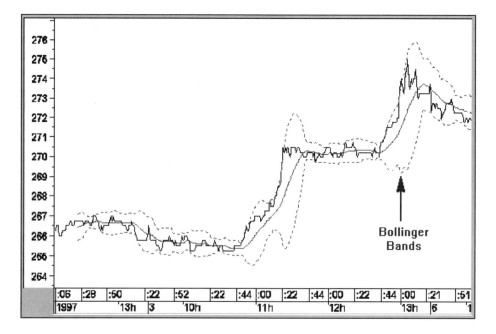

Question 27

Knowing that technical analysis is not perfect and deals in probabilities, in this chart, is the price more likely to rally before a major down move takes place?

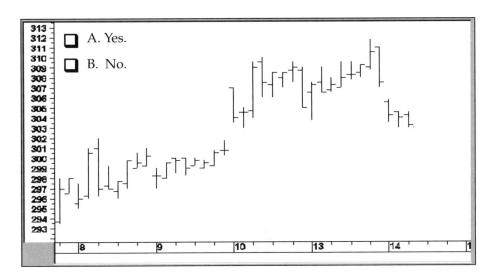

A. Yes.

B. No.

Question 28

Circle the best point to place a stop for the liquidation of a long position. The stop should indicate a trend reversal has taken place.

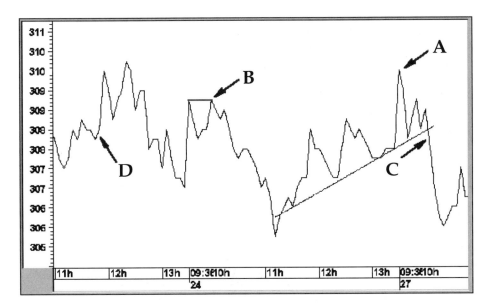

Question 29

Which of these statements is correct?

☐ A. Trading success is inversely related to emotional stimulation.

☐ B. Trading success is directly related to the number of trades that can be done in a day.

☐ C. Trading success is only possible with low commissions.

☐ D. Trading success is more achievable with emotional stimulation.

Question 30

You should:

☐ A. Continue trading no matter how you feel so you do not lose touch with the market.

☐ B. Get really over-margined when you feel good about the markets because that is when you are likely to be the most successful.

☐ C. None of these answers are correct.

☐ D. Only trade when there is an opportunity and you feel good about it.

Question 31

Circle the letter that is the outside bar.

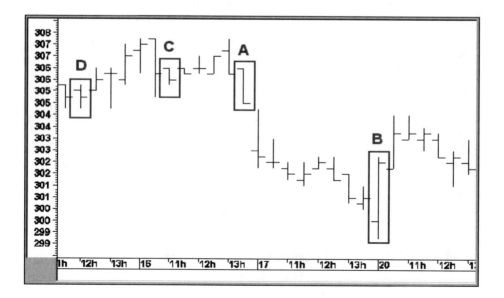

Question 32

Circle the letter that is the inside bar.

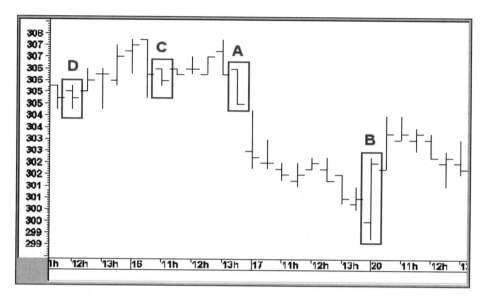

Question 33

Circle the combination that is a two bar reversal.

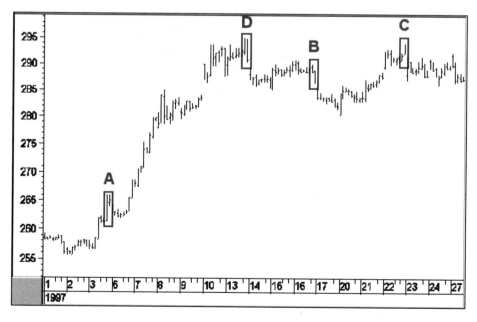

Question 34

If a stock fails to rally after a better than expected earnings report:

    ☐ A. It is now likely to decline.

    ☐ B. It will probably advance when people realize that the earnings are good.

    ☐ C. It will move sideways until the next report pushes it up or down.

    ☐ D. None of the above.

Question 35

It is better to trade an illiquid market because:

    ☐ A. It moves faster so you can make more money.

    ☐ B. The pros do not like illiquid markets so it's easier for you to trade them.

    ☐ C. None of these answers are correct because the statement in the question is not correct either.

    ☐ D. Breakouts are easier to spot.

Appendix

Quiz Answers

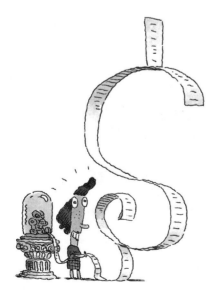

Question 1

      A. No, C is the correct answer.

      B. No, C is the correct answer.

☑   C. Yes, this is the correct answer.

      D. No, C is the correct answer.

Question 2

☑   A. Yes, this is the correct answer.

      B. No, A is the correct answer because gaps are usually, but not always, filled.

      C. No, A is the correct answer.

      D. No, A is the correct answer.

Question 3

☑   A. Yes, this is the correct answer.

      B. No, you should always place liquidation stops for long positions below support.

Question 4

      A. No, D is the correct answer.

      B. No, D is the correct answer.

      C. No, D is the correct answer.

☑   D. Yes, this is the correct answer.

Question 5

      A. Although partially correct, C is the more complete answer.

      B. Although partially correct, C is the more complete answer.

☑   C. Yes, this is correct.

      D. No, C is the correct answer.

Question 6

    A. Although partially correct, D is the more complete answer.

    B. Although partially correct, D is the more complete answer.

    C. Although partially correct, D is the more complete answer.

    ☑ D. Yes, this is the correct answer.

Question 7

    A. No, D is the correct answer.

    B. Although partially correct, D is the more complete answer.

    C. Although partially correct, D is the more complete answer.

    ☑ D. Yes, this is the correct answer.

Question 8

    ☑ A. Yes, this is the correct answer.

    B. No, A is the correct answer.

    C. No, A is the correct answer.

    D. No, A is the correct answer.

Question 9

    A. Although partially correct, D is the more complete answer.

    B. No, D is the correct answer.

    C. Although partially correct, D is the more complete answer.

    ☑ D. Yes, this is the correct answer.

Question 10

    A. No, D is the correct answer.

    B. No, D is the correct answer.

    C. No, D is the correct answer.

    ☑ D. Yes, this is the correct answer.

Question 11

    A. Although partially correct, C is the more complete answer.

    B. No, it should be placed at an appropriate support or resistance level. This could be an actual price level, near a trendline or a moving average.

☑ C. Yes, this is the correct answer.

    D. No, C is the correct answer because a stop should be placed at an appropriate support or resistance level. This could be an actual price level, near a trendline or a moving average.

Question 12

    A. Although partially correct, D is the more complete answer.

    B. Although partially correct, D is the more complete answer.

    C. No, D is the correct answer.

☑ D. Yes, this is the correct answer.

Question 13

    A. No, a retracement should normally fall between 1/3 to 2/3 of the previous advance.

☑ B. Yes, this is the correct answer because a retracement should normally fall between 1/3 to 2/3 of the previous advance.

Question 14

☑ A. This is correct because the rally retraces more than 1/3 of the previous decline.

    B. This is incorrect because the rally retraces more than 1/3 of the previous decline.

Question 15

    A. No, C is the correct answer.

    B. No, C is the correct answer.

☑ C. Yes, this is the correct answer.

    D. No, C is the correct answer.

Question 16

A. No, B is the correct answer because the RSI trendline break develops from an overbought condition.

☑ B. Yes, this is the correct answer because the RSI trendline break develops from a neutral reading.

Question 17

A. Although partially correct, D is the more complete answer.

B. Although partially correct, D is the more complete answer.

C. Although partially correct, D is the more complete answer.

☑ D. Yes, this is the correct answer.

Question 18

A. No, B is the correct answer.

☑ B. Yes, this is the correct answer.

C. No, B is the correct answer.

D. No, B is the correct answer.

Question 19

A. No, C is the correct answer, because it is the longest time span.

B. No, C is the correct answer, because it is the longest time span.

☑ C. Yes, this is the correct answer.

D. No, C is the correct answer, because it is the longest time span.

Question 20

A. No, B is the correct answer.

☑ B. Yes, this is the correct answer.

C. No, B is the correct answer.

D. No, B is the correct answer.

Question 21

      A. No, even though the price can move higher, the odds do not favor this happening. C is the correct answer.

      B. No, even though the price can move lower, the odds do not favor this happening. C is the correct answer.

☑ C. Yes, this is the correct answer.

      D. No, C is the correct answer.

Question 22

      A. No, there is no such thing.

☑ B. Yes, this is the correct answer because there is no such thing as a perfect indicator.

Question 23

☑ A. Yes, if things are going to go wrong, it will usually happen when you are positioned against the main trend.

      B. No, the odds do not favor profits from a contra-trend move.

Question 24

      A. Although partially correct, D is the more complete answer.

      B. Although partially correct, D is the more complete answer.

      C. No, D is the correct answer.

☑ D. Yes, this is the correct answer.

Question 25

☑ A. Yes, this is the correct answer.

      B. No, A is the correct answer.

      C. No, A is the correct answer.

      D. No, they are calculated from standard deviations not simple moving averages. A is the correct answer.

Question 26

     A. No, the bands are narrowing the only conclusion we can come to that a sharp price move may be forthcoming. There is no indication here as to which direction it will be. C is the correct answer.

     B. No, the bands are narrowing the only conclusion we can come to that a sharp price move may be forthcoming. There is no indication here as to which direction it will be. C is the correct answer.

☑ C. Yes, this is the correct answer.

     D. No, the bands are narrowing the only conclusion we can come to that a sharp price move may be forthcoming. There is no indication here as to which direction it will be. C is the correct answer.

Question 27

☑ A. Correct, because there is a gap, and gaps are usually filled reasonably close to their formation.

     B. No, this is incorrect, because there is a gap, and gaps are usually filled reasonably close to their formation.

Question 28

     A. No, this is above the previous high. At this point there is no indication that the trend has reversed. C is the correct answer.

     B. No, this is at resistance. It's a good place to sell, but there is no indication that the trend has reversed. C is the correct answer.

☑ C. Yes, this trendline represents support, so a break of the support is a good point to place a stop.

     D. This is just above the previous low, which could well turn out to be support. This is not a good point to place a stop. C is the correct answer.

Question 29

☑ A. Yes, this is the correct answer.

 B. No, A is the correct answer.

 C. No, A is the correct answer.

 D. No, A is the correct answer.

Question 30

 A. No, D is the correct answer.

 B. No, D is the correct answer.

 C. No, D is the correct answer.

☑ D. Yes, this is the correct answer.

Question 31

 A. No, D is the correct answer.

 B. No, D is the correct answer.

 C. No, D is the correct answer.

☑ D. Yes, this is the correct answer.

Question 32

 A. No, B is the correct answer.

☑ B. Yes, this is the correct answer.

 C. No, B is the correct answer.

 D. No, the high is the same level as the previous bar's high. It is not therefore completely inside that bar. B is the correct answer.

Question 33

 A. No, D is the correct answer.

 B. No, D is the correct answer.

 C. No, D is the correct answer.

☑ D. Yes, this is the correct answer.

Question 34

☑ A. Yes, a stock or market that fails to respond to good news is highly suspect.

   B. No, a stock or market that fails to respond to good news is highly suspect. A is the correct answer.

   C. No, a stock or market that fails to respond to good news is highly suspect. A is the correct answer.

   D. No, a stock or market that fails to respond to good news is highly suspect. A is the correct answer.

Question 35

   A. No, C is the correct answer.

   B. No, C is the correct answer.

☑ C. Yes, this is the correct answer.

   D. No, quite the reverse. C is the correct answer.

KST Formulas

	ROC	MA	Weight	ROC	MA	Weight	ROC	MA	Weight	ROC	MA	Weight
5-Minute Bar Short-term	6	10	1	10	10	2	15	8	3	20	15	4
5-Minute Bar Long-term	60	30	1	90	40	2	120	60	3	200	100	4
15-Minute Bar Short-term	10	10	1	15	10	2	20	10	3	30	15	4
15-Minute Bar Long-term	30	15	1	45	20	2	60	30	3	90	45	4
Short-term Tick	12	10	1	20	10	2	30	8	3	40	15	4

MetaStock Professional Real-time Formulas

5-Minute Bar Short-term KST
(Mov(ROC(C,6,%),10,S)*1)+(Mov(ROC(C,10,%),10,S)*2)
+(Mov(ROC(C,15,%),8,S)*3)+(Mov(ROC(C,20,%),15,S)*4)

5-Minute Bar Long-term KST
(Mov(ROC(C,60,%),30,S)*1)+(Mov(ROC(C,90,%),40,S)*2)
+(Mov(ROC(C,120,%),60,S)*3)+(Mov(ROC(C,200,%),100,S)*4)

10/15-Minute Bar Short-term KST
(Mov(ROC(C,10,%),10,S)*1)+(Mov(ROC(C,15,%),10,S)*2)
+(Mov(ROC(C,20,%),10,S)*3)+(Mov(ROC(C,30,%),15,S)*4)

10/15-Minute Bar Long-term KST
(Mov(ROC(C,30,%),15,S)*1)+(Mov(ROC(C,45,%),20,S)*2)
+(Mov(ROC(C,60,%),30,S)*3)+(Mov(ROC(C,90,%),45,S)*4)

Short-term Tick KST
(Mov(ROC(C,12,%),10,S)*1)+(Mov(ROC(C,20,%),10,S)*2)
+(Mov(ROC(C,30,%),8,S)*3)+(Mov(ROC(C,40,%),15,S)*4)

Glossary

A

Accumulation - A characteristic of a market bottom where smart money is said to be buying from uninformed hands. Accumulation takes place against a negative news background. Accumulation also applies to the basing process in chart patterns or formations. It is the first of three phases in a major trend, the other two being markup and distribution.

B

Basis Points - A measure for the yield on any security; one basis point equals 0.01% of the yield. For example, if an interest rate or yield moves from 6% to 6 .25% it is said to rise by 25 basis points.

Breakout - A price move that takes a security beyond a specific measurable benchmark. Examples would be a moving average crossover, trendline violation, or price pattern completion.

C

Chande Momentum Oscillator (CMO) - The Chande Momentum Oscillator (CMO) was developed by Tushar Chande, a scientist, inventor, and respected trading system developer. Tushar Chande developed the CMO to capture what he calls "pure momentum." It is closely related to, although unique from, other momentum oriented indicators such as the RSI, Stochastic, Rate-of-Change, etc. It is most closely related to Welles Wilder's RSI (see Relative Strength Index).

Confirmation - An indication that two or more price series or indicators are in agreement. Originally used in Dow theory where the Dow Jones Industrials confirmed trend movements in the Rails (now Dow Jones Transportation Average).

Consolidation - A congestion area that follows a strong trend, either up or down. In a rising market, a consolidation represents a temporary battle between buyers and sellers prior to the resumption of the uptrend. In declining markets, a consolidation is followed by a resumption of falling prices.

Continuation Pattern - A price pattern in which prices trade in a sideways range prior to resuming the prevailing trend.

D

Day Traders - Speculators who take positions in futures or options contracts and liquidate them prior to the close of the same trading day.

Distribution - Develops after a price rise where so-called smart money is expecting a decline and sells to uninformed or unknowledgeable buyers who are not.

Divergence - When two or more price series and/or indicators fail to show confirming trends. Negative divergences occur at market peaks, while positive divergences develop at market bottoms. The significance of a divergence is a direct function of its size; i.e., over time, the question is whether there is a series of divergences between the indicators and the number of indicators that are diverging.

Double Bottom - A price reversal pattern following a prolonged decline. It consists of two lows that develop around the same level. The second should be accompanied by considerably less volume than the first. The pattern is completed when the price rallies above the high separating the two lows. This breakout should be accompanied by relatively heavy volume.

Double Top - A price reversal pattern following a prolonged rally. It consists of two peaks that develop at approximately the same level. The second peak is usually accompanied by less volume than the first. The pattern is said to be completed when the price breaks below the low separating the two bottoms.

E

Envelope - Lines surrounding an index or indicator, that is, trading bands.

Equilibrium Line - A line that is frequently plotted on oscillators to reflect neutral momentum.

F

Flags - Short-term consolidation formations that develop during rallies. These patterns are constructed by drawing two approximately parallel trendlines connecting the peaks and troughs. Flags are said to fly at half-mast because they often develop halfway up a price move.

G

Gap - A period (usually a day) in which the daily range is completely above or below the previous period's trading range. It is said that the "market abhors a vacuum." Consequently it is normal for gaps to be "filled" reasonably soon after they have been "opened."

H

Head and Shoulder Bottoms - A final decline (the head) separated by two smaller declines (the left and right shoulders). When the price rallies above a line joining the two shoulder rally highs, the pattern is completed. It is important for the breakout to be accompanied by relatively heavy volume.

Head and Shoulders Tops - Price patterns that consist of a final rally (the head) separated by two smaller rallies (the left and right shoulders). When the price breaks below the reaction levels flagged by the two shoulders, the pattern is completed. Head and shoulders usually offer reliable signals.

I

Inside (day) Bar - A day in which the daily price range is completely within the previous day's daily price range. It indicates a balance between buyers and sellers and, if preceded by a worthwhile trend often represents a short-term reversal signal.

Inverse Head and Shoulders Patterns - Consist of a final decline (the head) separated by two smaller declines (the left and right shoulders). When the price rallies above a line joining the two shoulder rally highs, the pattern is completed. It is important for the breakout to be accompanied by relatively heavy volume.

K

Key Reversal Day - A day in which, following a strong trend, the price opens sharply in the direction of the then prevailing trend. By the end of the session the price closed close to the previous day's close, or even below it. Key reversal days are exhaustion phenomena and are typically accompanied with heavy volume.

KST (Know **S**ure **T**hing) - An oscillator developed by Martin Pring calculated from the weighted summed rate of change of 4 smoothed rate of change indicators. KST's can be calculated for any time frame, including Intraday. The most common are short, intermediate and long-term (Primary trend). KST's can also be very effectively applied to comparative relative strength.

L

Leverage - Controlling large dollar amounts of a commodity with a comparatively small amount of capital.

Limit Order - An order to buy or sell above or below a fixed price.

Limit price Moves - A restriction on the maximum amount a futures price can fluctuate in a given period (usually a day).

M

Margin - In stock trading, an account in which purchase of stock may be financed with borrowed money; in futures trading, the deposit placed with the clearinghouse to assure fulfillment of the contract. This amount varies daily and is settled in cash.

Margin Call - The demand upon a customer to put up money or securities with a broker. The call is made if a customer's equity in a margin account declines below a minimum standards set by the exchange or brokerage firm. This happens when there is a drop in price of the securities being held as collateral.

Market Order - Instructions to a broker to immediately sell to the best available bid or to buy from the best available offer.

Momentum - Measures the speed or velocity of a price move. It is a generic term embracing all types of oscillators. Examples include the rate-of-change, MACD, RSI, Stochastics, etc. All oscillators, to some extent or another, are subject to the same interpretive principles. The most common are overbought/oversold readings and positive and negative divergences.

Moving Average - A mathematical procedure to smooth or eliminate the fluctuations in data and to assist in determining the underlying trend. The principal varieties are simple, exponential, weighted, variable and triangular. It is calculated by adding the prices for a predetermined number of days and then dividing by the number of days.

N

Negative Divergence - When two or more averages, indices or indicators fail to show confirming trends.

O

Opening Range - The range of prices that occur during the first 30 seconds to fifteen minutes of trading, depending on the preference of the individual.

Oscillator - An indicator used to identify overbought and oversold price regions.

Outside Day (Bar) - A day in which the trading range completely encompasses that of the previous session. It is often a signal that market psychology has changed and therefore represents a short-term reversal signal. Outside "days" (bars) can also be observed for Intraday, weekly and monthly data.

Overbought Condition - A high momentum, or oscillator, reading that indicates prices have moved too far from the norm; i.e., that the probabilities favor a trend reversal.

Oversold Condition - A low momentum, or oscillator, reading that indicates prices have moved too far from the norm; i.e., that the probabilities favor a trend reversal.

P

Pinocchio (bar) Day - One in which the bulk of the trading takes place outside the range of the high and low, as well as the range for several previous sessions. Pinocchios represent exhaustion whipsaw moves and can develop in up or down markets.

Position - Market commitment. A *buyer* of a futures contract would be in a long position and, conversely, a *seller* of futures contracts would have a short position.

Price Patterns - When a trend reverses direction, the price action typically traces out a formation known as a reversal pattern. The larger and deeper the pattern, the greater is its significance. Patterns that are formed at market tops are called distribution formations; i.e., the stock or market is assumed to be undergoing distribution from strong, informed hands to weak, uninformed buyers. Price patterns at market bottoms are known as *accumulation formations*. Price formations may also represent temporary interruptions of the prevailing trend, in which case they are called *continuation patterns*.

R

Rally - A brisk rise following a decline or consolidation of the general price level of the market.

Rate of Change (ROC) - A momentum indicator in which today's closing price is divided by the closing price *n* periods ago. Multiply by 100. Subtract 100 from this value.

$$(C\ today/Cn) * 100) - 100$$

Rectangles - Horizontal trading ranges where buyers and sellers are evenly matched. They can be reversal or consolidation price patterns and develop in up and down trends.

Relative Strength Index (RSI) - A momentum indicator developed by J. Welles Wilder and used among other things to ascertain overbought/oversold readings and divergences. The RSI can be calculated for any time span, but 14 periods is the accepted default. Overbought and oversold lines are generally plotted at 70 and 30 for this time span.

Resistance - A concentration of supply sufficient to halt a rally.

Retracement - A price movement that develops in the opposite direction from the prevailing trend.

S

Saucer Base - Similar to a cup and handle formation, but the saucer base is shallower and rounder in shape and is not associated with the cup.

Selling Short - Selling a security and then borrowing it with the intent of replacing it at a lower price. Selling short in a futures market occurs when the trader enters a position by assuming responsibility of the seller.

Short Covering - The process of buying back stock that has already been sold short.

Short Selling - Short selling is normally a speculative operation undertaken in the belief that the price of the shares will fall. It is accomplished by borrowing stock from a broker in order to sell shares one does not own. Most stock exchanges prohibit the short sale of a security below the price at which the last board was traded.

Stop-Limit Order - A stop order variation in which a trade must be executed at the exact price or better. If the order cannot be executed, it is held until the stated price, or better, is reached again.

Stop Order - An order to buy or sell when the market reaches a specified point. A stop order to buy becomes a market order when the futures contract trades (or is bid) at or above the stop price. A stop order to sell becomes a market order when the futures contract trades (or is offered) at or below the stop price.

Support - A concentration of demand that is sufficient to temporarily halt a downtrend.

T

Technical Analysis - The art of identifying a trend reversal at a relatively early stage and riding on that trend until the weight of the evidence proves that the trend has reversed.

Tick - The minimum fluctuation of a tradable security.

Tick Indicator - Measures the number of stocks traded on a specific exchange whose last trade was an uptick or a downtick.

Time Limit Order - An order that designates the time during which it can be executed.

Trading Range - A period in which prices fluctuate within specific price levels. A trading range reflects an overall balance between buyers and sellers.

Trailing Stop - A stop-loss order that is continually changed to follow the prevailing price trend.

 Trend - The tendency of a set of statistical data as related to time to move in a specific overall direction.

Trendline - A line drawn that connects a series of highs in a downtrend or a series of lows in an uptrend. Up trendlines represent support and down trendlines resistance. Trendline penetrations either result in consolidation moves or an actual reversal in trend. Their significance is determined by their length, the number of times they have been touched or approached and the steepness of the angle of ascent or descent.

Two Day (bar) Reversal - These patterns develop after a persistent trend. The first opens on the low (high in a downtrend) and closes on the high (low in a downtrend). The second opens at the same level as the previous session's close and then closes at, or close to, the previous session's low (high in a downtrend)

V

Volatility - A measure of a stock's tendency to move up and down in price, based on its daily price history over the latest 12 months.

Volume - Calculated for a specific period of time, it is the number of purchases or sales made of a commodity futures contract. Often used to refer to the total transactions for one trading day.

W

Whipsaw - A buy or sell signal from any technical indicator that is quickly invalidated.

Technical Support

Installation Instructions:

This CD has an Autorun feature. Insert CD into CD-ROM drive and the CD will start automatically. Please allow sufficient time for this to load.

If the Autorun feature does not work, follow the instructions in the Support document found on the CD to turn this feature on. Or, you can insert the CD into your CD-ROM drive and double-click on the Setup.exe icon. Then access the program by clicking on START, PROGRAMS, PRING and locate the "DAY TRADING" icon in the flyout.

1. We recommend not changing the default directory.
2. This program is best viewed using small fonts.
3. This CD is best viewed in 800 x 600 pixels and 256 colors.
4. For additional support, please read the Support file on the CD.

To access the Support guide located on the CD-ROM:

1. Right-click on the Start button and left-click on Explore.

2. Locate your CD-ROM drive and double-click on the file called Support.

3. This file can be viewed in WordPad or Word 2000. If you cannot access either of the files, please visit our site and access the file by going to: http://www.pring.com/support1.htm.

Additional support issues and updates can be located at http://www.pring.com/support.htm. ■

SYSTEM REQUIREMENTS: The CD contained herein is a Win/NT-based product only. Minimum System Requirements: Pentium 166 or higher, SoundBlaster compatible sound card, updated video card.

Index

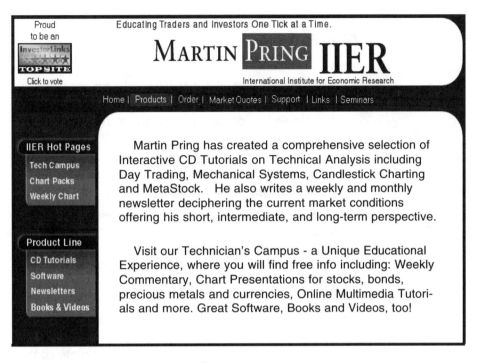

Technician's Guide to Day Trading

This set of two, 4-hour tutorials on momentum and oscillator interpretation goes beyond Martin Pring on Market Momentum as the "ultimate" momentum source, with quiz.

Principles of Momentum Interpretation and Four Popular Indicators $69.95

This 4-hour CD covers numerous techniques for interpreting momentum indicators, from overbought/oversold and divergences, to advance breakdowns and breakouts, extreme swings, mega overboughts and oversolds; how short-term momentum indicators can also be used to identify primary trend reversals, and why it is important, even for short-term traders, to know the direction of the main trend. Illustrated with marketplace examples using intraday, to long-term time frames, finer points of the RSI, Stochastic, MACD and Rate of Change indicators are discussed. For intermediate traders and above.

Advanced Momentum Indicators $69.95

The Advanced CD moves on to explain the theory, methods of interpretation and strengths and weaknesses of a host of momentum indicators including the Directional Movement System, Parabolic, Commodity Selection Index, Chaikin Money Flow, Trix, Demand Index, Herrick Payoff, Volume Oscillator, Volume Rate of Change, Linear Regression, Indicator and Slope, Chaunde Momentum Oscillator (CMO), Dynamic Momentum Indicator, Relative Volatility Indicator, Relative Momentum Index, Klinger Oscillator, R-squared Price Projection Bands and Oscillator, Inertia Forecast Oscillator, Qstick, Aroon. All in all, there are over 23 different indicators in. For intermediate traders and above.

Combo Price $119.95

To order, or learn about other products by Martin, please visit our web site at:

http://www.pring.com

Breaking the Black Box

Learn How to Design, Test and Apply Mechanical Trading Systems Using Profitable Examples with this 3-hour CD-ROM course and 284-page book.

Martin's ***Breaking the Black Box*** is a user-friendly CD for traders and investors who want to design and apply their own automated or mechanical trading systems. Part 1 of this nearly 3-hour audio-visual presentation takes you systematically through the process of designing, testing and applying systems in the market place, along with tools for risk management, leverage, timing and more. Part 2 and 3 build on these principles with actual market place examples of several tried and tested systems.

Part 2 covers systems based on a single security, such as U.S. equity market, Closed mutual funds, soybeans and the CRB. Part 3 highlights intermediate relationships. Here, you will learn to analyze equities vs. short-term interest rates, CRB vs. gold, bonds vs. commodities and systems which use relative strength.

Even the best systems eventually come apart and this course offers some guidelines on how to check for failure before it becomes too costly.

An index enables you to quickly isolate any of the subject matter. A quick click on the topic of your choice and the lesson is immediately played. ***Breaking the Black Box*** is the ideal resource to perfect your trading skills.

Finally, ***Breaking the Black Box*** comes complete with an interactive quiz, an excellent way to strengthen newly learned skills. Once you have taken the quiz, the program stores your results and you can easily follow your progress.

> "I found it to be excellent, full of good ideas, comments and insights."
> *- B. Cromwell*

$69.95

Introduction to Technical Analysis

A comprehensive 8 1/2 hours of interactive CD training and accompanying 288-page workbook, designed for the beginner to intermediate technician.

Every chapter is full of animated diagrams, eye-catching animated reinforcements and real marketplace movies - so concepts are learned, applied and retained.

Technical Analysis Explained, now in its 3rd edition, was the foundation for this unique concept, but Martin took this project a step further by breaking it down so that even a newcomer to technical analysis will be able to pick up the information quickly and apply it to real market situations.

> "I applied some of the chart analysis to get out of positions in the NASDAQ. You saved me over $5,000 last week!" - *J. Chang*

Every chapter has an interactive quiz designed to strengthen newly acquired skills. The 288-page workbook is an excellent quick and easy reference source. A complete table of contents and in-depth index on the CD lets you locate topics instantly.

> "This is a great book for the beginners. It explains in a simple language and easy flow and maintains the interests of the novice. I would recommend this book, it is a small investment, for making analysis before buying stocks." - *H. Garcha, Baton Rouge, LA*

$49.95

Learning the KST

Learn to apply the theory behind this unique indicator for your short-, intermediate- and long-term analysis.

Martin Pring's *Learning the KST* provides you with perspective because it helps identify those elusive short-term swings in the futures markets and time-sensitive decisions within your investment portfolios.

The KST is a unique indicator which can be used by both traders and investors. Traders like it because it helps identify those elusive short-term swings in the futures markets. Investors like it because it helps with those time-sensitive decisions within their investment portfolios. However, the most valuable function of the KST is its ability to provide you with perspective.

You've seen market-oriented commercials which make wild claims about perfect indicators, new systems, black boxes and so forth. The KST doesn't need to make extravagant claims - developed more than 10 years ago, the KST system was successful in identifying the 1990 bottom in the bond market (as featured in an article in the December 10, 1990 issue of *Barron's*) and the 1995 peak in the Deutsche mark.

In *Learning the KST* you will discover the concept behind this useful indicator, together with its strengths and weaknesses, all in more than a dozen full-color movies and accompanying charts and illustrations.

Following the 2-hour presentation, you will find a 40-question interactive, multimedia quiz to help you understand what you have learned. The automatic scoring system allows you to compare the results of up to three tests so you can monitor your progress.

$69.95

Introduction to
Candlestick Charting

Complete guide to candlestick charting includes Western charting, Renko, Kagi and 3-Line Break. A step-by-step introduction with market examples.

Martin Pring's *Introduction to Candlestick Charting*, is a comprehensive 4-hour CD tutorial, designed for all levels of technicians.

Over 4 hours of multimedia, interactive instruction provides a solid grounding in this exciting field of technical analysis. Within its 10 chapters, you'll be introduced to the basics of Candlestick construction, how to identify and interpret Dojis, Morning Star, Hammers, Tweezer Tops, Tasuki Gaps and more. There's also a complete chapter dedicated to Candlesticks and Western charting.

All 10 chapters are complemented by colorful diagrams, animated theory reinforcements and real marketplace movies - so concepts are learned, applied and retained.

An interactive quiz at the end of each chapter strengthens new skills automatically keeps your current and two previous scores.

$69.95

To order, or learn about other products by Martin, please visit our web site at:

http://www.pring.com

or call:
800-221-7514 or 941-364-5850

Notes

PLEASE READ <u>BEFORE</u> OPENING CD PACKET

Software and Information License Agreement

The software and information on this CD-ROM(s) (collectively referred to as the "Product") are the property of The International Institute for Economic Research, Inc ("IIER") and are protected by both United States copyright law and international copyright treaty provision. You must treat this Product just like a book, except that you may copy it into a computer to be used and you may make archival copies of the Products for the sole purpose of backing up our software and protecting your investment from loss.

By saying "just like a book," IIER means, for example, that the Product may be used by any number of people and may be freely moved from one computer location to another, so long as there is no possibility of the Product (or any part of the Product) being used at one location or on one computer while it is being used at another. Just as a book cannot be read by two different people in two different places at the same time, neither can the Product be used by two different people in two different places at the same time (unless, of course, IIER's rights are being violated).

IIER reserves the right to alter or modify the contents of the Product at any time.

This agreement is effective until terminated. The Agreement will terminate automatically without notice if you fail to comply with any provisions of this Agreement. In the event of termination by reason of your breach, you will destroy or erase all copies of the Product installed on any computer system or made for backup purposes and shall expunge the Product from your data storage facilities.

Limited Warranty

IIER warrants the physical CD-ROM(s) enclosed herein to be free of defects in materials and workmanship for a period of fourteen days from the purchase date. If IIER receives written notification within the warranty period of defects in materials or workmanship, and such notification is determined by IIER to be correct, IIER will replace the defective CD-ROM(s). Send request to:

Customer Service, IIER
1539 S. Orange Avenue, Sarasota, FL 34239

The entire and exclusive liability and remedy for breach of this Limited Warranty shall be limited to replacement of defective CD-ROM(s) and shall not include or extend to any claim for or right to cover any other damages, including but not limited to, loss of profit, data, or use of the software, or special, incidental, or consequential damages or other similar claims, even if IIER has been specifically advised as to the possibility of such damages. In no event will IIER's liability for any damages to you or any other person ever exceed the lower of suggested list price or actual price paid for the license to use the Product, regardless of any form of the claim.

IIER SPECIFICALLY DISCLAIMS ALL OTHER WARRANTIES, EXPRESS OR IMPLIED, INCLUDING BUT NOT LIMITERD TO, ANY IMPLIED WARRANTY OF MERCHANTABIL-ITY OR FITNESS FOR A PARTICULAR PURPOSE. Specifically, IIER makes no representation or warranty that the Product is fit for any particular purpose and any implied warranty of merchantability is limited to the fourteen day duration of the Limited Warranty covering the physical CD-ROM(s) only (and not the software or information) and is otherwise expressly and specifically disclaimed.

This Limited Warranty gives you specific legal rights; you may have others, which may vary, from state to state. Some states do not allow the exclusion of incidental or consequential damages, or the limitation on how long an implied warranty lasts, so some of the above may not apply to you.

This Agreement constitutes the entire agreement between the parties relating to use of the Product. The terms of any purchase order shall have no effect on the terms of this Agreement. Failure of IIER to insist at any time on strict compliance with this Agreement shall not constitute a waiver of any rights under this Agreement. This Agreement shall be construed and governed in accordance with the laws of Florida. If any provision of this Agreement is held to be contrary to law, that provision will be enforced to the maximum extent permissible and the remaining provisions will remain in force and effect.